Training and Development

George Green

- *The* fast track route to mastering all aspects of training and development

- Covers key training and development best practice and thinking, from establishing current levels of knowledge and skills to setting priorities, and from developing individual action plans to using technology

- Examples and lessons from some of the world's most successful businesses, including American Airlines and National Air Traffic Services, and ideas from the smartest thinkers, including Meredith Belbin and Katherine Briggs and Isabel Briggs Myers

- Includes a glossary of key concepts and a comprehensive resources guide

PEOPLE

09.10

>EXPRESS EXEC.COM<

essential management thinking at your fingertips

The right of George Green to be identified as the author of this work has been asserted in accordance with the Copyright, Designs and Patents Act 1988

First published 2002 by
Capstone Publishing (A Wiley Company)
8 Newtec Place
Magdalen Road
Oxford OX4 1RE
United Kingdom
http://www.capstoneideas.com

CIP catalogue records for this book are available from the British Library and the US Library of Congress

ISBN 1-84112-250-5

Printed and bound in Great Britain

This book is printed on acid-free paper

Substantial discounts on bulk quantities of Capstone books are available to corporations, professional associations and other organizations. Please contact Capstone for more details on +44 (0)1865 798 623 or (fax) +44 (0)1865 240 941 or (e-mail) info@wiley-capstone.co.uk

Contents

Introduction to ExpressExec

ExpressExec is 3 million words of the latest management thinking compiled into 10 modules. Each module contains 10 individual titles forming a comprehensive resource of current business practice written by leading practitioners in their field. From brand management to balanced scorecard, ExpressExec enables you to grasp the key concepts behind each subject and implement the theory immediately. Each of the 100 titles is available in print and electronic formats.

Through the ExpressExec.com Website you will discover that you can access the complete resource in a number of ways:

» printed books or e-books;
» e-content – PDF or XML (for licensed syndication) adding value to an intranet or Internet site;
» a corporate e-learning/knowledge management solution providing a cost-effective platform for developing skills and sharing knowledge within an organization;
» bespoke delivery – tailored solutions to solve your need.

Why not visit www.expressexec.com and register for free key management briefings, a monthly newsletter and interactive skills checklists. Share your ideas about ExpressExec and your thoughts about business today.

Please contact elound@wiley-capstone.co.uk for more information.

Introduction to Training and Development

Looks at the role of training and development in the modern world of business. It considers the following.

» The growing recognition by organizations of the importance their people play in their success.
» Why training and development are important.
» The importance of training and development to each individual, whether manager or junior.
» The application of the concepts to any type of organization.

Tom Peters and Robert Waterman (1982) talk of "productivity through people" in their book *In Search of Excellence*. Charles Handy (1989) in *The Age of Unreason* talks of people being treated as "assets, requiring maintenance, love and investment."

In this modern era most organizations recognize the truth contained in these statements and understand that if they are to be successful, it will be through the efforts of their people.

New technology is constantly being developed to give companies a competitive edge. However, most technology needs people to operate it and there are three crucial points to be borne in mind:

» the technology itself can usually be matched by competitors sooner or later;
» the technology is only as good as the people who operate it; and
» there are usually people somewhere in the process between the technology and the end customers of the organization.

It will follow, therefore, that those organizations which train and develop their staff, both in the effective use of the technology and in how to interact with customers, are likely to gain a competitive edge on those which only invest in the technology.

As a result, most successful organizations regard the training and development of their staff as a matter of most importance.

Turn to the mission statement of any company that you care to think of and you will be sure to find a reference about how it intends to help its staff develop and grow.

Some organizations take this a step further and have their own centers of excellence where training and development are carried out.

» McDonald's, the US restaurant chain, has its Hamburger University in Illinois, where it trains its staff in the basics of the company's operations.
» British Airways has several Quest centers throughout the world, devoted to distance learning.
» Biolink, a group of scientific companies in the south of England, have come together with academic partners to provide a virtual university for their members, where they can access a library and other resources via their own intranet.

We will learn more about these in Chapters 4 and 5.

As we will also see later, many other organizations support their staff by funding training and development programs which often lead to qualifications.

A key point here is that training and development should be available for everyone in the organization to the extent that they need it. The senior manager in a large organization may well benefit from completing an MBA, but the Saturday morning part-time worker also needs to know how to carry out their job effectively and to interact with any customers they may meet. The training for the latter may be far less complex and intensive than the former, but it is just as important.

Some would say it is even more important because it is not usually the chief executive who meets the organization's regular customers on a consistent basis.

Of course, the organization stands to benefit considerably from the investment it puts into its training and development activities. If they are focused effectively, they should have a beneficial effect on the bottom line.

All of the points mentioned above will apply to any organization, whether it is commercially driven or a not-for-profit organization, like a charity or a government department.

We will be looking in more detail, in Chapter 6, at how the benefits that result from training and development can be evaluated.

To illustrate the importance of training and development in today's competitive environment, Singapore Airlines uses the same type of language as Handy when it talks of being "committed to recruiting and nurturing bright and dynamic individuals." Its investment in employee training forms the largest component of its operating expenditure.

What Are Training and Development?

Explores what people mean when they talk about training and development. It considers the:

» definition of training and development
» differences between training and development
» links with motivation
» links with performance management
» training needs analysis
» training objectives
» methods of training
» who drives training and development?

So, what do we mean when we talk about training and development? And why are they always mentioned together?

There are generally considered to be three main aspects to training and development:

» knowledge
» skills
» attitude.

The three go together and all of them need to be addressed if a person is to make an effective contribution to their organization.

> "Cognitive learning no more makes a manager than it does a swimmer. The latter will drown the first time he jumps into the water if his coach never takes him out of the lecture hall, gets him wet and gives him feedback on his performance."

When he said this, Henry Mintzberg (1975), the celebrated writer and theorist on management issues, was stressing the need for budding managers to practice their skills in real situations as well as seeking knowledge from a book or from a series of lectures.

We could add that, unless Mintzberg's swimmer has a positive attitude and wants to swim, he won't even jump into the water at all.

So training and development are all about letting people gain knowledge, practice their skills, and hone their attitudes. The three aspects together are often referred to as competence. We will be looking at competence approaches to training and development in more detail in Chapter 6.

TRAINING OR DEVELOPMENT?

Training and development are usually linked together; but what's the difference between them?

» **Training**, with its focus on excellence, relates to the knowledge, skills, and attitude that people need to do their current job in its current form, with its current level of responsibility.

» **Development**, with its focus on growth, relates to the knowledge, skills, and attitude people need to do their next job or a different form of their current job, usually with greater responsibility.

Most successful organizations will strike a balance between training and development, ensuring that they have people who are very capable of carrying out their current jobs, while also preparing them to take on new tasks and new responsibilities.

We will also see, in Chapter 3, that there has been, in the last few years, a move both toward experiential learning (learning by doing) and toward focusing on the outcomes of training, that is, the way in which people behave after the training has been completed. It may be, therefore, that we should be talking neither of training nor development, but rather of "learning."

LINKS TO MOTIVATION

The psychologist Abraham Maslow (1943) and the theorist Frederick Herzberg (1964) both recognized the importance of development in motivating people. Self-esteem and self-actualization were at the top of Maslow's hierarchy of human needs, while Herzberg identified responsibility, advancement, achievement, recognition and the work itself all as motivating factors.

Training and development will help people to achieve and to grow and are, therefore, powerful forces in motivating people and ensuring that they remain with the organization.

LINKS TO PERFORMANCE MANAGEMENT

In fact, most organizations will embed training and development into their performance management or appraisal systems. An individual's performance will be managed by giving them regular feedback. Periodic reviews, usually three monthly, six monthly, or yearly, formalize the process. Training needs for their current role will be identified during this process and arrangements made for them to be addressed. Development needs for the individual's future role are also mapped out.

The process of identifying training and development needs and setting out strategies to fulfill them is usually referred to as training needs analysis (TNA).

TRAINING NEEDS ANALYSIS

This can be carried out in respect of:

» an individual, as mentioned above
» a team or department
» the whole organization.

Whichever is chosen, the process is essentially the same. Let's look at each level.

The individual

The starting point is to look at the skills, knowledge, and attitudes that are needed for the person to do their job effectively.

This is compared to the knowledge, skills, and attitudes that the individual currently has. If the individual meets the levels required for their job, then they are fully competent; however, if they don't, then there is a gap between what they have to achieve and what they are currently achieving, which is known as the training gap.

The person will probably not be lacking or deficient in all of the knowledge, skills, and attitudes that their job requires; rather there will be certain areas where further training is needed. The usefulness of the training needs analysis is in the fact that it identifies these specific areas and allows specific strategies to be put in place to address the gaps.

The team or department

Each different type of job in the team or department will have a different mix of knowledge, skills, and attitudes.

All of the jobs will be analyzed to identify the composite levels of knowledge, skills, and attitudes needed. This can be compared to the levels displayed by the people in the team and the gap is established.

For example, a sales team of six people in a travel agency may need at least four people to have detailed knowledge of how to use a computer reservation system (CRS). It may also need to have four people trained in fares and two in accounts. Everyone needs to be trained in customer service skills. In this very simplified example the current levels are given in Table 2.1 (where a tick shows that the person has the particular knowledge or skill).

Table 2.1

Person	CRS	Customer service	Fares	Accounts
F	✓	✓	✓	
J		✓	✓	
S	✓	✓		
L	✓	✓		✓
P		✓		
T		✓	✓	
Total actual	3	6	3	1
Total needed	4	6	4	2
Gap	1	0	1	1

There is clearly a gap which requires at least one person to be trained additionally in fares, CRS, and accounts. All are already satisfactorily trained in customer service skills. The agency can now set out its training strategy to fill these gaps.

The organization

This exercise is similar to that for the team or department, but it covers the whole organization and is, therefore, quite a complex exercise, especially in large organizations.

DEVELOPMENT NEEDS ANALYSIS

Although we have been talking about training needs here, development needs can be identified in the same way. An organization which is going through a great deal of change will, for example, identify areas of knowledge, skills, and attitudes that it has little need for now but will in the future. It can, therefore, set out a strategy to ensure that it has them in sufficient quantities when the changes take place. For example, a financial services company that does not offer mortgages at present, but makes a decision that it will in future, will need to set out a training program for its current staff or employ some new staff who already have the necessary knowledge and skills.

There is another specific type of training that we should mention here, which is induction training.

INDUCTION TRAINING

This is often referred to as "orientation" because its purpose is to enable the new entrant to find their way around the organization. It will cover areas such as:

» introductions to their manager and colleagues
» health and safety policy
» equal opportunities policy
» fire precautions
» first aid arrangements
» smoking policy
» links to other departments and head office
» administrative arrangements such as desk or equipment allocation.

An example of an organization that recognizes the importance of induction training is the Taj Group of hotels in India and the Far East. They ensure that all of their staff, whether they interact on a regular basis with customers or not, know the layout and who is responsible for what in the hotel in which they are working. This ensures that, if they do meet customers who are seeking advice or have a problem, they have the knowledge to enable them to seek help on the customer's behalf.

TRAINING OBJECTIVES

We can see that the training needs analysis will result in training strategies, either individual or departmental, which all have a specific purpose: that is, to bring about improvement in a specific area of knowledge skills or attitudes. They all, therefore, have an objective, which the organization can meet.

Once the organization has carried out the training or development it can evaluate whether it has been successful, though we will see later, in Chapter 6, that the evaluation process will need to have been considered at an earlier stage.

METHODS OF TRAINING

There are a huge number of training methods available to an organization, as included in Table 2.2.

Table 2.2

Group work	One to one	Individual work	Organizational
Action centered	Mentoring	Individual research	Job shadowing
Role plays	Coaching	Work assignments	Attachments
Presentations	Giving instruction	Practice	Job swaps
Case studies		Internet	Networking
Group discussions		Tapes	Company intranet
Learning support groups		CD-ROM	
Lectures			
Videos			

Succession Planing. (handwritten)

We will look at which might be most effective in certain situations in Chapter 6.

WHO DRIVES TRAINING AND DEVELOPMENT?

Training and development have come to be recognized as activities that bring enormous benefits to an organization. In the past they might have been driven by a personnel or human resources department which set out courses and offered them to the various departments of the organization. In the modern era, however, they tend to be:

» driven by business needs;
» led by line managers rather than the human resources department; and
» linked to the overall success of the organization.

It might be envisaged, then, that everyone would regard training and development as very worthwhile activities.

Despite this, the old adage, " if money is tight, cut down on training," does still exist to some extent. There are several reasons for this.

» Training often means taking a person from the workplace.
» If there is a choice between letting down the customer and carrying out training, the customer will always win.
» There is a perception that a short-term cut in training will not affect the long-term needs of the business.
» Sometimes all of the training requirements are not written into the organizational budget.

For all of these reasons, there has been a significant move toward using training methods which reduce costs to a minimum and keep people in the workplace as much as possible, while remaining very effective. Open learning approaches, which we will cover in more detail in Chapters 3 and 6, and the e-revolution which we will look at in more detail in Chapter 4, can be combined to produce very cost-effective training and development solutions.

KEY LEARNING POINTS

» The key elements of training and development are, knowledge, skills, and attitudes.
» Training focuses on a person's current role.
» Development prepares people for future roles.
» Training and development are inextricably linked to motivation and performance management.

» A training needs analysis allows training to be targeted where it is most needed.
» Induction or orientation is vital for new entrants.
» Training objectives should be agreed before training commences.
» There are a variety of training and development methods.
» Training is now likely to be driven by the needs of the organization.

The Evolution of Training and Development

An analysis of how the concepts have evolved. It includes:

- » reinforcement theories
- » cognitive theory
- » evaluation
- » competency approaches
- » experiential learning
- » team development
- » self-development
- » mentoring
- » coaching
- » open learning.

In this chapter we can explore how the concepts relating to training and development have evolved. All of the theories have contributed to the ways in which training and development are practiced today, so no one theory can be regarded as having all of the answers.

There were originally two main schools of thought among psychiatrists about how people learned, at the beginning of the twentieth century:

» **stimulus–response theory**, as demonstrated by the experiments of Pavlov (during the latter part of the nineteenth and early twentieth centuries) and Skinner (in the early part of the twentieth century), which suggests that people can be conditioned into a particular type of behavior; and
» **cognitive theory**, as suggested by the Swiss psychiatrist Jean Piaget in 1928, which indicates that, rather than simply responding to stimuli, the brain will process information in some way and its reasoning powers and perception will affect the person's behavior; feedback from others will play an important part in the process.

Later in the twentieth century, from the 1960s, it began to be recognized that it was important to evaluate how effective an organization's training and development activities were; Donald Kirkpatrick developed his four-stage plan.

From this time, organizations also started to develop competency approaches and carry out training needs analyses as we saw in Chapter 2.

Also during the 1960s, it was suggested that people could learn by simply taking part in an activity, which led to experiential learning, as proposed by Kolb *et al.* (1979) and Honey and Mumford (1986).

From the 1980s there has been a great emphasis in team development, as analyzed by Professor Meredith Belbin, who identified nine natural team roles; most successful organizations today will have a reference to the importance of team working in their mission statement.

In the late 1980s and 1990s there was a huge amount of work devoted to self-development, as proposed by Tony Buzan (1986), among others, who looked at many ways in which individuals can improve their own learning powers.

Finally, the 1990s have seen a large rise in the people involved in mentoring and coaching, and open learning.

We can identify the time line shown in Table 3.1.

Table 3.1

Pavlovian classical or response reinforcement	from 1880s
Skinnerian operant reinforcement	from 1930s
Cognitive theory	from 1930s
Behavior modification	from 1950s
Evaluation theories	from 1950s
Competency approaches	from 1950s
Kolb's learning cycle	from 1974
Belbin's team roles	from 1981
Learning styles	from 1989
Self-development	from mid 1980s
Mentoring and coaching	from 1990s
Open learning	from 1990s

Let's look at these in a bit more detail.

STIMULUS–RESPONSE THEORY

The Russian psychiatrist Ivan Pavlov is famous for his work with dogs during the late nineteenth century. He began by showing food to a dog (the stimulus), which resulted in the dog beginning to salivate (the response). He experimented by ringing a bell before showing the dog the food. After he had done this several times, the dog began to salivate when it heard the bell. It had now been conditioned to salivate in response to the bell.

Humans, too, respond to the sight of food. We can also be conditioned. For example, we find ourselves salivating as we come in sight of our favorite restaurant, long before we see or smell any food! This is usually referred to as classic or response conditioning.

There is another type of conditioning which is referred to as operant conditioning. This examines how different behaviors can be established by reinforcing them with rewards.

Burrhus Frederic Skinner carried out some work with rats. He put a hungry rat in a cage containing a lever, which, when pressed, would deliver a small piece of food to the rat. As the rat moved haphazardly around the cage, it would, at some point, touch the lever and obtain the food. Every time the rat did this the behavior was reinforced by it receiving more food; gradually, it learned to depress the lever more and more.

So, it was argued that reinforcement could be used with humans and by rewarding desirable behaviors, or by not rewarding (or even punishing) undesirable behaviors, human behavior could be changed.

The work of Pavlov and Skinner, among others, led to a behavior modification approach in schools, universities, and industry from the late 1950s onwards, especially in the United States. Industry used it to improve things like timekeeping or work rate. Various rewards were applied ranging from additional money to a simple thank you.

However, it was found that, once the reinforcement ceased, then the desired behaviors ceased too, so reinforcement needs to be either continuous or, at least, intermittent if it is to have the desired effect.

COGNITIVE THEORY

Cognitive theory takes almost the opposite view in the sense that it points to the importance of the brain in the learning process.

For example, we might see food that we don't perceive as being very nice and we won't start salivating; clearly, the brain has processed some additional information here, which has resulted in a different response.

Jean Piaget focused mainly on the psychology of children and his main quest was to find out how knowledge grows. However, his work had a widespread effect, as it showed that knowledge grows progressively from childhood through to adulthood. The adult's logic and ways of thinking are very different from and much more powerful than a child's. It seemed logical, therefore, that the brain, in the way it perceives things and in the way it processes information, is very much involved in the learning process. Much of the learning will come from social interaction.

Here we can concentrate on:

» feedback
» observation
» making choices.

Feedback

Feedback from others will play an important part in the cognitive learning process.

J. Luft and H. Ingham (1955) produced their Johari (Joe and Harry) window which clearly demonstrates that we see ourselves quite differently from the way in which others see us. They identified four different areas in the mind:

» **open area** – which is shared with both the individual and other people;
» **hidden area** – which consists of things we know about ourselves, but are not prepared to share with other people;
» **blind spot** – where there are things that other people know about us, but we just can't see them ourselves; and
» **the unknown area** – where there are things that no one knows about, neither ourselves nor others; this is often called the id.

Clearly, feedback from others will help us to reduce the blind spot and help us to learn more about ourselves and the way we do things. Learning in groups with other people will allow us to obtain feedback on what we're doing.

It is also important to note that there are some cultures in which people have a relatively small open area, which means that they are very reticent about sharing their thoughts with other people.

Fons Trompenaars, in his book *Riding the Waves of Culture* (1993), identifies cultures as specific or diffuse. Specific cultures (like some in the United States) will tend to share a lot of their inner selves with others, even relative strangers, and they may actively seek feedback. Diffuse cultures (like some in Japan) will only share a small amount of their inner selves with strangers and are likely to share more only when they have become very much more acquainted with the person concerned; they are less likely to seek feedback. Clearly this has implications for trainers who might be intending to set up learning groups.

Observation

Watching what others do will also be important in the cognitive learning process. If we identify role models who carry out a particular task or job to the highest standards, we can watch how they do it and try to do it in the same way.

Making choices

Making choices about the way we want to do things is also a part of the process. Just because we are told that something is done in a certain way, it doesn't mean we can't find a different way.

The American psychologists Katherine Briggs and Isabel Briggs Myers recognized that everyone has a different approach to the way in which they:

» gather information;
» make decisions;
» relate to other people; and
» allocate priorities.

They developed a test to analyze a person's different preferences in these areas, which would reveal how they might act in various situations. We will look at this in more detail in Chapter 8.

Both the cognitive and the conditioning approaches appear to fit with the work of the motivation theorists that we met in Chapter 2, such as Maslow and Herzberg.

» The cognitive approach clearly relates to Herzberg's motivators and to Maslow's higher needs for humans to stretch themselves further and further to greater and greater achievement.
» The reinforcement approach seems to relate more to the lower needs in Maslow's hierarchy, which are physiological, security, and social needs.

EVALUATION

We saw, in Chapter 2, that training and development often suffer when resources are stretched and are often seen as the lowest business priority. In the 1960s a lot of work was carried out to try to find a way to evaluate the benefits that training and development bring. Much of the work is still valid today and many organizations use the same methods that were first identified then. We can look briefly at the work of two key people here, namely D.L. Kirkpatrick and A.C. Hamblin.

Kirkpatrick set out a method for evaluating the effectiveness of an organization's training and development activities. The ideas were developed in 1959 and published in 1967 and they can be found in full in his book, *Evaluating Training Programs: The Four Levels* (2nd edn 1998). The four levels are:

» **Reaction** – how do people feel during and immediately after the training?
» **Learning** – how much have they learned in terms of knowledge skills and attitudes?
» **Performance** – what are they now doing differently as a result of the learning experience?
» **Organizational results** – what additional benefits has the organization gained?

Hamblin (1974) adds a fifth level:

» **Ultimate value** – has the training helped the organization meet its strategic mission and goals, in terms of profitability, growth, or survival?

We will be looking in more depth at evaluation in Chapters 6 and 10 and in particular at Donald Kirkpatrick in Chapter 8.

COMPETENCY APPROACHES

Organizations began to want a formal method of working out what skills they needed to run their business and to ensure that those skills were available. The approach is extremely popular in the modern era, with many organizations linking training and development with human resource planning and recruitment. One of the key factors in a competency approach is that an organization focuses more on the outcomes of the training than on the inputs to it. Earlier approaches tended to evaluate the methods used in training, while competency approaches evaluate the differences in people's behavior as a result of the training. We will look at competency approaches in more detail in Chapter 6.

EXPERIENTIAL LEARNING

Popular figures in experiential learning were Kolb and Honey and Mumford.

Kolb *et al*. identified the learning cycle, which is the various stages that an individual goes through when they are learning. They are:

» having an experience;
» reflecting on it;
» forming abstract concepts and generalizations; and
» testing the implications of these concepts in different situations.

Then the cycle begins again.

Peter Honey and Alan Mumford (1986) built on the Kolb learning cycle, suggesting that each person will have a preference for one or more of these stages. Some people will like the actual experience itself but will not want to reflect on it. Others will prefer to watch someone else do something and then reflect on it and make observations. They identified four learning styles which reflected these preferences.

» Activist – who prefers having the experience. *Do*
» Reflector – who likes to reflect upon what has happened. *Watches*
» Theorist – who conceptualizes and develops theories.
» Pragmatist – who experiments by testing the concepts out in new situations.

We will look at learning styles in more detail in Chapter 8. In the process of experiential learning, trainers act more as facilitators, a role in which they help people to learn, rather than give instructions or information.

TEAM DEVELOPMENT

It has been recognized that there is much to be gained by people working effectively together in teams. In fact, the mission statements of most successful organizations stress the importance of team working.

Meredith Belbin, in his work *Management Teams: Why they succeed or fail* (1981), identified nine team role types.

» Coordinator – who makes a good chairperson and ensures that everyone in the team has an opportunity for input.
» Shaper – who will drive the team forward.
» Plant – who will provide the creativity.
» Implementer – who will get things done.
» Monitor evaluator – who will ensure that all options are considered.
» Team worker – who will help cement the team together.
» Resource investigator – who develops outside contacts.
» Completer/finisher – who will finish things off.
» Expert – who will provide specific areas of knowledge.

He found that each individual was predisposed toward one or more of these types as their natural role in the team; people would also have secondary roles that they could perform if there was a need.

Many organizations recognize the value of having good team-working arrangements. Team days out and team weekends have become a familiar factor in training, both as motivational events and as methods for developing team and interpersonal skills.

As early as 1965, B.W. Tuckman had identified four stages of team development.

» Forming – when the team first comes together.
» Storming – when conflicts arise.
» Norming – when the team begins to settle down to business.
» Performing – when the team really begins to shine.

We will look at this model in more detail in Chapter 8.

SELF-DEVELOPMENT

There has been a real focus on self-development during the last 10 to 15 years. The key concepts tend to be related to:

» positive mental attitude;
» disposing of "baggage from the past;"
» being more creative;
» identifying a career path;
» doing what you want to do;
» developing the mind; and
» keeping the body healthy.

Key writers here include Tony Buzan, who first developed the idea of mind mapping, and Stephen Covey, who set out the seven habits of highly effective people in his book of the same name (1990). We will meet them in Chapter 8.

One very interesting development in the context of self-development is the growing application of neuro-linguistic programming, often referred to simply as NLP. This was developed in the 1970s by Richard Bandler and John Grinder, but has taken time to enter the mainstream of training and development. This approach helps people to communicate more effectively with other people and also to overcome their own personal barriers, thus building self-belief and self-confidence. We will look at this in a little more detail in Chapter 8.

MENTORING AND COACHING

Mentoring and coaching are seen by many organizations as two of the most effective methods of developing staff. Let's look briefly at each in turn; we will consider them in more detail in Chapter 6.

Mentoring

The first mentor appears in Homer's *Odyssey*; he was the elder statesman left behind by Odysseus to look after the family and, in particular, his son Telemmachus. It is from this figure that the term has been handed down.

A mentor can be a terrific support to an individual during their development. Indeed, the main roles are to counsel and support. Mentors are usually at a more senior level in the organization than the person whose mentor they will be and are likely to have a more strategic role.

Coaching

Coaches differ from trainers in that they usually work on a one-to-one basis with an individual, rather like the tennis coach working with one or more players. Various organizations regard coaching in different ways. In Chapter 6 we will be looking at a model which identifies four main forms of coaching.

» The instructor – who demonstrates how things are done.
» The watching brief – who monitors performance.
» The guide – who gives direction and feedback.
» The empowerer – who delegates and supports.

The circumstances in which each might be used are analyzed in Chapter 6, where we will also look at the role that coaches can play in helping people work out their individual action plans.

OPEN LEARNING

Open learning was developed as a response to the need to reduce the overall costs of training and development. One of the biggest elements of cost was the fact that people were away from their workplace to attend a training course or event. This could lead to lost production or to increased costs in covering their duties.

Open learning involves people studying on their own at their own pace. It is often supported by a limited number of workshops. The learner is provided with a tutor to support them and is also given workbooks, tapes, videos, software, or Internet packages. The attraction for organizations is that the person spends relatively little time away from their job.

KEY LEARNING POINTS

The evolution of training and development included the following concepts:

» Pavlovian classical or response reinforcement
» Skinnerian operant reinforcement
» Cognitive theory

» Behavior modification
» Evaluation theories
» Competency approaches
» Kolb's learning cycle
» Belbin's team roles
» Learning styles
» Self-development
» Mentoring and coaching
» Open learning.

The E-Dimension

The Internet presents new opportunities. Chapter 4 explores the key issues, including:

» how the new technology is used in training and development from the perspectives of:
   » the organization
   » the team
   » the individual
» tracking training and development
» case study: PowerGen.

We can now look at some of the opportunities that the e-dimension offers to organizations in their training and development activities. We can consider these opportunities from the following perspectives:

» organizational
» team
» individual.

ORGANIZATIONAL

Many organizations now have their own intranet, which is similar to the Internet but will usually be accessible only to employees of the organization. It is possible to include many items of latest news to keep staff up to date with what is going on both inside and outside the business. Courses can be advertised and new initiatives explained.

Training materials can be purchased or designed in electronic format, bringing the organization considerable savings. Instead of buying or designing a hundred workbooks, for example, it can provide the materials on the intranet and staff can access them from their desk computers. Staff may not even need to print the materials out. The staff don't have to carry weighty books around with them and they can even print off short sections which they can read easily on the train to and from work, say, if they are interested.

The organization can also target a particular training item specifically to the individual who needs it. For example, instead of having to provide a full workbook, the person may need only one or two sections, which can be downloaded or printed off by the person concerned.

Training materials can also be made available to remote staff, especially in large, global organizations, where they might have to be out of the workplace for several days, for instance to attend a traditional training event.

The intranet can be particularly useful when an organization is going through a significant change program and it is important that all of the staff have access to some of the new initiatives that are being introduced. It allows everyone to know what is going on at the same time, which can be very important if employees are spread over a wide geographic area.

Many organizations maintain their own libraries of reference materials which people can access for research and development purposes. They may even have their own virtual university. For example, Biolink, a group of scientific companies in the south of England, have joined with academic partners to provide a virtual university for their members, where they can access a variety of resources connected to management development, including a set of one-page fact sheets on 100 different management topics, each of which can be printed out as a manager's topic for the day.

Also in the UK, the Chartered Insurance Institute (CII) has joined with Reuters Business Insight to provide a wide range of reports of interest to the financial services industry, which are being made available on the CII Library On Line (CIILO).

American Airlines has its own flagship university, based at Fort Worth in Texas, where it provides training and development for a wide range of staff across a variety of methods, including computer and Internet-based training programs.

The UK financial services company Egg has launched a virtual university, where its staff can have access to training and development from around the world, using the Internet.

Lockheed Martin, based at Bethesda, Maryland, research, design, and develop advanced technology systems for a wide range of industries including space, aeronautics, telecommunications, and defense. It has a very hi-tech approach to training. For some of its programs it provides multimedia packages, including student guides, instructional materials, lesson plans, test packages, and video, animation, and presentations which can be sent out electronically and delivered to a person's computer. They can then be linked to instructors for virtual classroom delivery of the program.

There are also training packages, such as Blackboard, for example, that enable organizations to set up materials and courses on the external Internet. They can be used to create courses, administer and track attendance, provide tutorial support, set up discussion rooms, and exchange messages.

Organizations can also access information and advice, via the Internet, from commercial consultants about current training and development issues, such as how to evaluate the effectiveness of their development methods. They can also usually find help from their industry institutes such as the CII mentioned above.

Clearly, for an intranet or the Internet to be effective, the organization does need to make it available to as large a number of staff as possible, by providing the necessary hardware and software. An example of an organization, PowerGen, that is taking a very innovative approach to this can be seen in the case study later in this chapter.

TEAM

From the team perspective, we can consider the advantages of the virtual classroom. People don't actually need to leave their workplace; they can attend the training event via their computer. They can also interact with other people undergoing the same training through the use of the following.

» **Online briefings** – in which each person receives the same information at the same time from the person who is facilitating the event. One particular advantage here is that, although they may receive the information at the same time as everyone else, they don't have to act on it at the same time. They can wait until their work pattern allows a convenient opportunity for them to focus on the item concerned. They can also make any required response in their own time too.
» **Discussion rooms** – which allow people to exchange ideas on relevant topics. They can be extremely useful for finding innovative approaches or for sharing experience. The rooms are usually facilitated by a trainer, though informal networks can also be very powerful in exchanging ideas. Discussion rooms can take several formats including:
  » real time, where several people are on line at the same time; and
  » notice boards, where messages can be posted and responded to one at a time as people log on to the program.
» **Conferencing** – in which meetings can be set up where people in remote places can both talk to and see each other, via the television screen, almost as if they were all in the same room. This allows more synergy between the attendees as they can spark ideas from each other. It also allows networking relationships to develop as they would at a traditional training event where people turn up in person.

INDIVIDUAL

There are many advantages to the individual, as follows.

» **Tutor support and help lines** – it is possible for learners to seek advice from their tutors or trainers on a one-to-one basis. This can be a very important aspect of any development program. Although a telephone conversation with a trainer is more personal and can offer a swift solution, the e-mail approach has some very distinct advantages. For example, it allows the trainer to:
  » consider their response more carefully;
  » carry out further research if the question demands it; and
  » send any advice of a general nature to other learners on the program.
» **Electronic delivery of assignments** – where a learner has to provide pieces of work such as exam papers, assignments, or projects; these can be submitted electronically, cutting down on administration and being delivered instantaneously. Feedback and marks can be sent back in the same way, thus allowing any errors or misunderstandings to be put right quickly.
» **Access to other learners** – learning networks can be a very effective way of sharing knowledge and experiences.
» **Working at their own pace** – people can work as quickly or as slowly as their own particular circumstances permit.
» **Working when it is convenient** – people can set aside time when they can choose to access the information and focus on it.
» **Quick responses** – turnaround of queries and feedback on submitted work is much faster via the Internet than by normal mail channels, especially when people are working at remote sites.
» **Easy access to information** – each individual has access to a wealth of information provided by the organization either through the intranet or via the Internet itself.

Although we have identified a wide range of opportunities that the e-dimension brings to learning, training, and development, the value of traditional methods should not be forgotten. If all training were to be carried out via the Internet, it would become a very sterile process.

People do benefit from interaction with others, both from the networking point of view and from the opportunity to exchange ideas, interpretations, and experiences; this does tend to work better when they can meet and talk to each other. After all, we have already seen, in Chapters 2 and 3, the importance of social interaction and feedback in the development process. When they meet, people can also give each other support and advice.

We also recognized, in Chapter 3, the value of experiential learning; this, too, can benefit from a group approach.

Experience with open learning programs suggests that people have a much better completion rate if they attend a number of workshops with other learners, as this helps to stimulate them.

The e-dimension, then, rather than as a substitute for traditional methods, should be seen as another additional set of tools that are available to an organization and to individuals, which, when combined with the more traditional methods, can provide powerful training and development solutions.

As well as the learning opportunities that we have mentioned above, the e-dimension can also provide opportunities for organizations to plan, manage, and track their training and development.

TRACKING TRAINING AND DEVELOPMENT

We saw, in Chapter 2, that it is very important that an organization identifies the knowledge, skills, and attitudes that it needs to carry out its business and plans to ensure that it can fulfill them.

A comprehensive software system like those provided by Work Smart, for example, can help.

» The organization carries out the analysis and identifies which jobs need which levels of knowledge, skills, and attitudes, and inputs these factors into the program. It can then enter the current levels for each of its staff. An overall gap will then be established and plans can be put in place to ensure that the gap for every individual in the organization is closed.
» As the training and development programs roll out and people gain the necessary qualifications and certificates or pass assessment criteria, their own personal skills levels are updated in the software program.

This might be particularly important in regulated areas such as the finance and safety-related industries, where specific skill levels have to be achieved for the organization to remain in business.

So, for example, if a new set of safety regulations were about to be introduced, the organization would identify those people who need to gain the new knowledge. A plan could be put in place to ensure they were fully trained before the legislation was introduced. As introduction day approached, the company could clearly identify any shortfalls and take steps to rectify the situation.

Any organization using this kind of planning and tracking system can clearly monitor progress toward complete fulfillment of its training and development needs. Managers and supervisors can use the tool to identify the needs of their own teams.

The data can also be accessed remotely, by authorized people.

There will usually be links through the system to specific training packages, such as special coaching on particular subjects, which can be accessed via the Internet too.

Let's now look at a particular company which has seen the potential of e-learning and is taking strategic steps toward its full introduction throughout the company.

CASE STUDY: POWERGEN

PowerGen is an Anglo-American integrated energy company. In the UK it provides electricity, gas, and telephone services to some 3.2 million customers and employs some 5000 staff. It claims to be the fastest growing of the major suppliers of utilities.

It has just made a decision to offer its staff a heavily subsidized package consisting of personal desktop computer, printer, software, and Internet connection. Staff will pay only some £8 per month for three years. The system, known as clicks@home, is not compulsory, but the company expects the take-up rate to be about 85 to 90%.

The aim is to cut the costs of administration in the company by changing many of the human resource activities into a self-service operation. This would include staff:

» updating their own personal records such as address details;
» claiming their expenses;

» checking salary and tax details;
» maintaining their own training records; and
» accessing their own training.

It may also allow an increase in people working away from the office and keeping in touch through their computer.

The idea is to let staff become so used to using the equipment at home that they will have no problems with using it at work.

There will be an e-learning program, which will allow staff to gain:

» tuition on how to use the Internet;
» tuition on office systems and routines; and
» access to Web-based training opportunities.

Instead of staff having to attend courses and take time out from work, most of their training needs will be available to them to access at their own pace and at the most convenient time. They will be able to do some learning during their own working hours and the company hopes this will stimulate them to supplement this by continuing their learning activities in their own time.

At the end of the three years the company hopes to upgrade the packages, though people will be able to buy their outdated equipment for a nominal sum and own it outright.

The company has been encouraged by a new government tax incentive scheme in the UK, which allows the use of computer equipment for personal purposes as long as the benefit in kind is below £500 per year, though this is not the main driver of the scheme.

Independent research commissioned throughout the UK, France, and Germany in May 2001 by PeoplePC, who are providers of such systems, suggested that less than 40% of the workforce in those countries have access to a personal computer or to the Internet either at work or at home.

Similar programs

Similar programs have been set up recently elsewhere in Europe, notably at the multimedia company Vivendi Universal in France; it has 110,000 employees in France and 150,000 other employees across several other countries, who will receive the system in due course.

In the United States, Ford Motor Company, American Airlines, Delta Airlines, and the New York Times have implemented similar schemes.

Back in the UK, the Leonard Cheshire Workability Project aims to provide free computer equipment, printer, software, and Internet access to certain unemployed, disabled people who have been hindered in their search for work. The aim is to enable them to learn new skills to help them find rewarding work. They will become registered students at a virtual college site on the Internet or with other local training organizations. They are allocated a personal tutor for their studies. Training in basic information technology applications will be offered to them and a network of expert volunteers will provide advice on setting up and using the equipment in their homes.

KEY LEARNING POINTS

» An intranet can be a powerful asset to an organization.
» Materials can be provided electronically.
» Team interaction is possible via personal computers.
» Individuals can access training in a very convenient manner.
» The use of e-learning should be combined with the best of traditional methods.
» Competence can be tracked via software programs.
» The provision of e-resources is the key to their wider use.

The Global Dimension

Looks at the application of training and development concepts in the global marketplace, including:

» cross-cultural approaches
» maintenance of standards
» interaction with learners
» use of technology
» case study: ExxonMobil.

In this chapter, we will look at training and development from a global perspective. Any organization that wants to operate in the global marketplace must take into account the diversity of people across the world. There is a myriad of different cultures, languages, customs, preferences, and expectations. Successful organizations recognize this and set out their strategies to take advantage of the opportunities it brings.

We can consider the following implications for training and development:

» cross-cultural approaches
» maintenance of standards
» interaction with learners
» use of technology.

CROSS-CULTURAL APPROACHES

The most successful organizations recognize the value of having a diverse workforce. Because so many of them work in a global environment, the advantages of employing people from a range of different cultures and languages are clear. They take every opportunity to bring people from different cultural backgrounds to share their training and development with others.

Let's look at how some companies do it.

Rolls-Royce, the company famous for aero-engines and marine power units, is a global business. Its head office is in Derby, UK, but it has units located throughout the world in Canada, the United States, Germany, France, Japan, India, Thailand, Indonesia, and Brazil. It ensures that its graduate entrants, who are planned to be its future senior managers, gain international experience by giving them overseas attachments after they complete their initial training. There is also a graduate exchange scheme between the UK and the United States. Part of their initial training is a cultural awareness program based in France.

Singapore Airlines offers those managers who show an aptitude the opportunity of managing overseas offices to gain international experience.

Qantas, the Australian airline, has a code share with British Airways, which means that the two airlines share the operations and revenue of their flights to and from the UK. Some staff in the Far East and Australia actually are employed by Qantas and also carry out work on behalf of British Airways. Some of Qantas's managerial staff from Singapore and the Philippines were able to attend a Certificate in Management course, which was being delivered by a British university and held in Sydney, for British Airways staff from various parts of Thailand, Australia, and New Zealand.

And it doesn't come much more cross-cultural than that!

In fact, British Airways takes a very positive approach to bringing cultural diversity into its training and development programs. The Certificate in Management course mentioned above was open to all junior/middle management and potential management staff throughout the world and was delivered mainly through open learning, which we met in Chapter 3. The course was supported by a number of workshops held in several regional locations throughout the world, including London, Delhi, Dubai, New York, Sydney, Paris, and Johannesburg.

The company also has a number of open learning centers throughout the world. They are called "Quest Centers" and give British Airways staff access to a wide range of books, videos, tapes, and interactive computer learning programs.

MAINTENANCE OF STANDARDS

One of the key challenges is to ensure that training and development are available so that employees can reach the same high standard in whichever country they may be working. Let's look at how some organizations achieve it.

McDonald's, the US restaurant chain, has its Hamburger University, which is located at Oak Brook, Illinois. Its 30 resident professors are responsible for training people in how to manage McDonald's operations. Translators and electronic equipment allow them to teach and communicate in 22 languages at one time. There are also Hamburger Universities in Japan, the UK, Germany, and Australia.

The Chartered Insurance Institute (CII) is an influential professional and educational organization in the global insurance and financial services industry. Although based in the UK, it has a strong presence in over 120 countries, with long-term affiliations with some 65 other institutes world-wide. Its aim is to deliver world-class standards of education and support to people working in the industry at every stage of their professional development. Some 10,000 of the CII's 64,000 members are based outside the UK. The CII provides examination centers in over 100 countries world-wide and supplies textbooks, training courses, and associate trainers to help people in the industry to work toward and pass their professional examinations. The CII has a range of international activities, all aimed at helping people throughout the world attain and maintain high standards in giving financial advice. It has been involved in seminars and conferences in locations such as Turkey, Russia, Bulgaria, Vietnam, and Slovakia.

Qantas and British Airways, which we mentioned earlier, also take a keen interest in maintaining standards of aviation and many of their competitors are able to use their flight simulators at Melbourne and Heathrow. Although, clearly, this access is allowed on a commercial basis, it does demonstrate the amount of global cooperation toward maintaining the high standards that exist in some industries, even among keen competitors.

Let's now consider some of the key implications for people who are involved in delivering training and development on a global basis.

INTERACTION WITH LEARNERS

Working globally presents a number of issues for the professional trainer when working closely with learners. Because people are so diverse around the world, strategies which work in one location or with one group of people may need to be changed for a different group. Strategies may also depend upon whether the group of people being trained is from the same cultural background or from several different ones.

We can consider the following key factors:

» language
» approach to learning
» perspectives
» experience
» communication
» comfort.

Language

The first decision will be to consider which languages are spoken by people in the group. If there is one that is predominant, then it may be the one used. If there is more than one, then the training may have to be carried out in several groups according to the language spoken.

Perhaps the real challenge arrives when people can communicate in the same language but have different levels of proficiency in it. This will usually be because it is their second or third language.

Trainers in these circumstances may need to beware of using too much idiomatic language, which may not always be understood. They may also need to check understanding more often.

They also need to consider, when learners with several different first languages are working in subgroups on role plays or case studies, which language(s) will used during the group discussion.

Written and audio/visual materials may also have to be made available in several different languages.

It may be possible for assignments or projects to be written in the first language and sent for assessment by tutors who speak that language.

The McDonald's approach of having a main center and several local centers appears to be a good strategy for overcoming a lot of these issues.

Approach to learning

Fons Trompenaars, in *Riding the Waves of Culture* (1993), makes the distinction between individualism and collectivism.

Individualists prefer to work and take responsibility as individuals. They may take the view that learning is an individual activity, which, when shared, will benefit the rest of the group; when working on case studies or solving problems, they might prefer to tackle the situation first on their own and then share their thoughts with the others in their group.

Collectivists, on the other hand, prefer to work and take responsibility in groups. They may consider that learning is a group activity and may prefer to tackle any situation as a group from the beginning.

A further distinction on the approach to training and development is that some people from certain cultural backgrounds are accustomed to being taught and, therefore, prefer a teacher, while others are accustomed to being allowed to learn for themselves, through research or activities, and, therefore, prefer a facilitator.

Perspectives

Learners from different parts of the world may have different perspectives on their experiences with the organization. A group of people from an organization's head office in New York may look at an issue differently from those in the branch office in Paris. The perspectives may be geographic, cultural, or hierarchical, or all three.

Experience

Learners from different global locations may have a completely different set of experiences. Tour representative based in Ibiza will have many different tales to tell from the representative based in Boston.

This can usually be used to advantage as people can learn from one another, through sharing experiences.

Communication

Trompenaars, mentioned above, identifies *diffuse* cultures in which people are unlikely to share their inner feelings until they know someone very well. Trainers may have to work hard to encourage them to open up and share their point of view with the other delegates. They may respond more to a one-to-one approach with a coach whom they can get to know and trust.

On the other hand, Trompenaars refers to *specific* cultures in which people may volunteer some very personal things about themselves. It may be difficult to stop them and they may dominate a group.

People from diffuse cultures are likely to set the context at some length before they actually make a particular point, which may cause other delegates to lose patience and to interrupt them. People from specific cultures, on the other hand, are likely to come directly to the point.

Comfort

It is important to recognize that different cultural groups may have different comfort needs if they are attending a training event. They may need to:

» dress in a particular way;
» eat from a vegetarian menu;
» carry out their prayers at certain times of the day; and
» observe religious festivals.

Let's now look at the ways in which new technology can help organizations to train people globally.

USE OF TECHNOLOGY

New technology makes it very much easier for global organizations to manage the training and development of their staff. Here are some examples:

» fast air travel shrinks distances that people travel to events;
» cheaper air travel reduces costs;
» e-mail reduces bulky training materials to pictures on a screen;
» e-mail makes arranging courses and conferences so much quicker;
» e-mail squeezes time differences – a message left at the end of a working day can receive a reply the following morning;
» e-mail allows amendments to course materials at the touch of a button;
» video-conferencing brings people together without them having to travel;
» video-conferencing allows a trainer to deliver a program across the world;
» computer-conferencing lets people exchange ideas at a distance;
» tele-conferencing lets people have a meeting without meeting;
» an intranet enables the whole workforce to gain access to resources;
» the Internet allows access to a world of external training opportunities; and
» text phones ensure people are easily contacted.

Each of these, individually, simplifies and reduces the costs of planning and delivering training and development programs in a global environment. Available all together they make very good friends indeed!

However, life is never that simple.

If an organization is operating globally, it may well be working in some of the developing countries where some of the technology is not available. This means that special arrangements need to be put in place to ensure that people are not left out of any of the arrangements:

» hard-copy materials and amendments may have to be sent by courier;
» messages may have to be faxed or telephoned;
» local trainers may need to deliver a program; and
» more face-to-face meetings may have to be arranged.

The most important issue here is to identify what technological resources are available and where they are at an early stage, so that appropriate strategies can be put in place.

Now let's look in more detail at a company that operates world-wide and see how it organizes its training and development.

CASE STUDY: EXXONMOBIL

In fact, we have two companies here because Exxon and Mobil recently merged to produce one very large petroleum and petrochemical company, which operates in over 200 countries around the world. Its main activities are:

» exploration and production of oil and gas;
» manufacturing of fuels, oils, and chemicals;
» electric power generation; and
» coal and minerals operations.

The company's headquarters are in Irving, Texas, and it has many regional offices around the world.

The responsibility for career development is considered to be shared between management, who provide challenging opportunities and coaching to improve performance, and the individual, who pursues opportunities to develop their skills and seeks feedback on how they are doing.

The company actively seeks a diverse workforce and takes great steps to provide a climate in which it can flourish. All employees receive training on appropriate and inappropriate behavior. Methods used include:

» formal training classes
» group sessions
» team-building activities
» lunch meetings with guest speakers
» newsletters.

There are local employee networks at locations around the world, where employees meet regularly on a voluntary basis to discuss shared experiences and to identify training opportunities. In addition, there are local mentoring and peer support programs.

There are also some 3000 people who work outside their home countries. The purpose of this is to transfer the skills that these people have to the local workforce as soon as possible. There is also a reverse trade-off in that the expatriates themselves grow in experience as a result of their posting, so the company wins both ways. They are also given training in cultural diversity as part of their development program.

We can now look at some specific examples of what the company is doing both in educating its employees and supporting the education of people around the world.

In Australia, there is a three-year graduate induction program, taking recruits from a variety of cultural and ethnic backgrounds. They are given training in a wide variety of topics readying them for their future careers, wherever in the world they may find themselves. They are offered career development workshops after one and three years.

In Nigeria, there is an apprentice training program, which teaches electrical, mechanical, instrumentation, and process skills; there is also a pre-apprentice program which allows people to improve their knowledge of science, math, and English before they begin the full program. The program is accredited through the UK and Canada.

There is a very interesting initiative in Germany, where training in oil spill prevention is given to heating oil resellers throughout the country.

A mobile van with a home heating oil system visits each of the resellers and a master driver delivers the training to them at their own location.

The company also sees itself as a global corporate citizen and supports many educational initiatives throughout the world.

For example, in Azerbaijan, which had used the Russian language until its independence, the company has worked with Azeri businesses and the relief agency Care to develop and print an Azerbaijani-English dictionary for elementary schools.

ExxonMobil clearly regards itself as a global company with global responsibilities. Its approach to training and development reflects this very well.

KEY LEARNING POINTS

» Most successful organizations recognize the value of a diverse workforce.

» Many organizations are operating globally.

» Cross-cultural awareness is an important part of training and development.

» When operating globally, it is vital to maintain training and development standards across the world.

» Trainers need to take cultural differences into account when delivering training events.

» New technology is extremely useful, though it may not be available everywhere.

The State of the Art

Examines the key debates, including:

» the role of training and development in change
» open learning versus traditional approaches
» competency frameworks
» coaching and mentoring
» methods of development
» evaluation: chicken or egg?
» educating the customer.

We can now examine some of the key debates in training and development. In this chapter we will be considering:

» the role of training and development in change
» open learning versus traditional approaches
» competency frameworks
» coaching and mentoring
» methods of training and development
» evaluation: chicken or egg?
» educating the customer.

THE ROLE OF TRAINING AND DEVELOPMENT IN CHANGE

In today's very competitive environment, people in organizations face a time of constant change. Charles Handy (1989) talks of "upside down thinking," while Tom Peters (1994) refers to the world as "topsy-turvy." In many cases the changes are significant and many people within the organization will find this uncomfortable. One of the main reasons for their discomfort may be that a different set of knowledge, skills, and attitudes may be needed for them to be successful in the new situation.

It is, therefore, important that, as part of the change in strategy, the organization provides the necessary training and development for its staff to enable them to feel confident to perform their changed roles effectively. Some examples of major change that will give rise to specific training and development needs are given in Table 6.1.

Changes to products and to legislation usually involve gaining some new knowledge and skills in addition to those that people already have. This is often very motivating and is seen as a challenge and an opportunity to do something different.

Changes to organizational structure, on the other hand, may mean that people change jobs completely and have to learn a whole new set of knowledge and skills. This can be a very difficult process for them and the quality of the organization's training effort will be very important both in retaining a person's effectiveness and their motivation. This effort will need to:

Table 6.1

Type of change	Training and development needs
New products	Technical training program to train employees to make or sell new products
Changing legislation, especially in safety, financial, or other regulated industries	Technical training program to train employees how to apply the new legislation
Changes to the structure	Training in new key responsibilities for each individual; organizational culture training
Growth of the organization	
Privatization of nationalized industries	Organizational culture and values training
Mission and values changes	

» offer staff the opportunity to develop new skills;
» help them cope with the process of change; and
» give awareness of the new organizational structure.

There may also be mergers between organizations with quite different cultural backgrounds, which present additional challenges and opportunities. Cultural training may be appropriate in these cases.

One of the most difficult changes that an organization can make, however, is to the organizational values and culture – because this means changing attitudes!

There are many examples of major changes to organizational culture, especially over the last 20 years or so when many organizations have faced increasing competition and have moved to a much more customer-focused culture.

Many organizations which were nationalized have been sold off by their governments to the private sector and have felt, for the first time, the teeth of competitors snapping at their heels. Their staff have had to learn a whole new way of interacting with customers who now have a choice about whether to use the organization's products or not.

It is not enough, however, simply to issue a new mission statement, setting out the new strategic objectives and values; such changes to the organization's vision need to be supported by training and development programs aimed at moving people to adopt new attitudes toward customers, colleagues, and other stakeholders.

Many organizations have responded by rolling out short course Customer First programs in which they provide a range of case studies and role plays, in which staff can learn about the vital importance of customers to the organization.

Others offer their staff opportunities to develop over a longer period by encouraging them to work towards qualifications, covering areas such as leadership, motivation, marketing, and customer service.

In these ways, the organization can achieve a critical mass for change in which the new attitudes become the norm and the old attitudes the exception.

OPEN LEARNING VERSUS TRADITIONAL APPROACHES

Most organizations have to control their costs very tightly. We saw, in Chapter 2, that training and development can often be the first activities to be sacrificed when resources are stretched.

Traditional approaches to training involve people attending courses, often for several days at a time. This incurs several types of costs including:

» travel costs
» hotel costs
» trainer provision
» room provision
» cover for the absent person
» course materials.

An open learning approach involves a self-study program for an individual in which the learner is provided with materials and works through them at their own pace, often in their own time. The costs involved here are:

» course materials, which might be downloaded via the Internet, an intranet, or e-mail; and
» provision of a support tutor by phone/e-mail.

Clearly, there is a significant saving in costs.

But can self-study be as effective as the traditional approach? Surely, as the cheaper option, it must be less effective?

Well, in fact, if we check out the advantages and disadvantages of the two approaches, we may find a fine balance between the two approaches, with each one having some significant factors going for it.

The traditional approach scores over open learning in the ways given in Table 6.2, whilst the open learning approach scores in the ways given in Table 6.3.

Table 6.2

Traditional learning	Open learning
Learners work in groups, leading to motivation and synergy	Learners work alone, no synergy, can lose motivation
Face-to-face tutor support may aid clarification	Remote tutor support, clarification may not be immediate
Allows group development as well as individual development	Allows individual development only
Very effective when large numbers of people must be trained quickly	Better for more sustained learning over a period of time

Both approaches allow:

» use of a variety of course materials
» use of new technology
» individuals to work toward qualifications, if they wish.

A very effective way of overcoming any of the disadvantages of the open learning approach and, at the same time, still allowing a very cost-effective solution, is to support it with a limited number of workshops spaced at intervals. This enables:

Table 6.3

Traditional learning	Open learning
Learners work at pace of group, which may be too fast for some and too slow for others	Learners work at own pace, allowing them to consolidate before moving on
No interim tutor support	Tutor support available at all times
Learner's skills develop mainly during courses	Learner's skills develop continuously
Distractions from others in the group	Focused on their own development
Learning activities are in company time	Individual can invest own time too

» synergy between individuals in the group;
» motivation to be increased;
» group development to take place; and
» clarification by tutors, face to face.

Many organizations, including Nestlé, British Airways, and the Civil Aviation Authority, use this approach for developing their junior managers.

When combined with some of the new technology such as e-mail, the Internet, intranets, computer-conferencing, and video-conferencing, this extended open learning approach can be very exciting indeed.

COMPETENCY APPROACHES

We noted earlier, in Chapter 2, that training and development are concerned with knowledge, skills, and attitudes. When an individual possesses all of the knowledge, skills, and attitudes they need to carry out their job effectively, they are described as competent.

Most jobs require the individual to be proficient in several different areas of knowledge, skills, and attitudes. It can, therefore, be useful to group these different areas together and call them competences.

For example, a manager in a manufacturing company may need quite different skills to chair meetings than to ensure that production targets are met – and different ones again to write effective operating reports. Table 6.4 is a very simplified example to illustrate the point.

Table 6.4

	Knowledge	Skills	Attitudes
Meetings	The current status of all items on the agenda	Presenting information	Assertive
	Responsibilities of the attendees	Listening to others	Valuing others
Production targets	Targets	Motivating others	Assertive
	Current position	Leading others	Customer focused
	Operating procedures	Agreeing performance targets	
	Problems		
Reports	Facts and figures relating to the topic	Clear writing style	Thorough
		Concise style	Thorough

In this example, the individual concerned can be quite clear about what knowledge, skills, and attitudes they need to perform the various aspects of their job. It is possible to be fully competent in some areas and not yet competent in others. The person in the table, for example, might be brilliant at achieving targets and managing meetings, but may need further development in report writing.

In this way, it is possible to build up a competency framework for all of the jobs in an organization. In a further refinement, it is possible to identify some jobs as having the same skills, knowledge, and attitudes, but at different levels.

So, our production manager might not need the same levels of report writing skills as a public relations (PR) manager who produces briefs on a daily basis to the managing director or to the press. Reasonably clear and reasonably concise might suffice for the production manager, whereas the PR manager might have to be very clear and very concise.

The latter may also need additional attitudes such as being assertive and customer focused.

Once the areas of competence are identified for each job and the levels of knowledge, skills, and attitudes for each of those areas are set out, the organization can begin the process of working out whether people are actually competent to carry out their jobs.

This is sometimes known as benchmarking. In this exercise, each person will usually assess themselves against the framework for their own job; their manager will also assess them (they may, for example, use a 1-10 scale). The results are compared in a joint approach and an agreed level is recorded. This is then compared to the levels that are required for the job.

This establishes any shortfalls in specific areas of knowledge, skills, and attitudes. Our production manager above, for example, may be found to meet or even exceed the required levels in report writing except that the reports are too long and need to be much more concise. This area of skills would now be identified as a training need and an action plan could be worked out by the individual and their manager to ensure that it is addressed within a certain time period. After this time, if the required rating is achieved, the individual can be declared fully competent.

This type of rating scale is a useful indicator of an individual's progress toward being fully competent at their job and provides an analysis of their individual training needs.

In some industries, the person may have to be assessed as competent before they can actually carry out the job and may have to demonstrate at regular intervals that they are maintaining that competence. This would apply in the financial services sector, where a person must be competent before they can give advice to customers, and in safety-related industries too.

One of the really significant changes brought by the interest in competency frameworks is that it forces people to look at the outputs of training and development rather than the inputs. In the past people would often be sent on courses because:

» "they could probably do with a course on that topic;"
» everyone else had attended it; and
» there were places available on it.

The scattergun effect suggested that if you sent people on enough relevant courses some of the learning would stick and the organization would probably have enough skills, somewhere, to carry out its business!

In the competency approach, however, the type of training needed is related specifically to the "gaps" identified between the levels of competence the person needs and the levels of competence that they are currently demonstrating; and they are specifically identified down to particular knowledge, skills, and attitudes.

The training provided is, therefore, driven by the changes in performance that are required (outputs) rather than what training courses are available. It can, therefore, be tailored specifically for that individual and will continue until the level of performance has improved.

The result of this, in turn, is that each person in the organization can have their own individual training and development plan. If they are already fully competent in all areas of their job, the main focus of the plan will be on maintaining that competence and developing new skills. If the person is not yet fully competent, the main focus of the plan will be to address the identified "gaps."

Let's now look at how the individual can work with coaches and mentors to fulfill their individual development plan.

COACHING AND MENTORING

First of all, we need to realize that it is not necessary to have a full competency framework. Any organization can set up a system in which its staff have individual development plans.

The key factor in the system is that the person will work with their coach, who may also be their manager, and work through a cycle of:

» identifying the knowledge skills and attitudes required;
» establishing the current levels being reached;
» establishing the gap;
» working out an action plan to address the gap;
» carrying out the action plan; and
» reviewing the new levels being reached.

Feedback is a key part of the learning process and the coach will employ the two types of feedback:

» motivational – to build up their confidence; and
» developmental – to build up their competence.

We identified, in Chapter 3, four main types of coach:

» the instructor
» the watching brief
» the guide
» the empowerer.

Many coaches will, in fact, use all four approaches at various times, according to the task and the individual concerned. It may depend upon:

» how much discretion the individual has in the way they carry out their job; and
» the current level of competence of the person concerned.

We can see, on the model shown in Fig. 6.1, four quadrants in which these methods might be used. It is the copyright of George Green and Bronwen Green and was first published in *Training and Competence News*, Autumn 2001. It is reproduced with kind permission.

» Individual with low level of discretion/low level of competence – the coach acting as instructor will work closely with the individual while they are at an early stage of the learning process and show them how to perform activities, often demonstrating by example; there will be relatively few ways of carrying out the task; review meetingss will tend to focus on how effectively the person followed the coach's lead when carrying out the task.
» Individual with low level of discretion/high level of competence – the coach acting as the watching brief will tend to let the person get on with the job because they are fully competent at it and have little discretion to try out any new ways of doing it. Regular reviews will be needed to ensure there is no complacency and these will tend to focus around motivational feedback; the individuals themselves

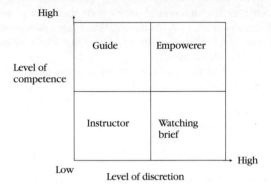

Fig. 6.1

might be considered for the role of coach/instructor as a means of further development.

» Individual with high level of discretion/low level of competence – the coach acting as guide will set small tasks and guide the individual through them in a fairly directive way at the outset; small tasks will allow for frequent feedback to be given as each is carried out. As the person's competence improves, the coach can set larger tasks and allow more discretion about how they are carried out; review meetings will tend to focus on how learning can be applied to more complex tasks.

» Individual with high level of discretion/high level of compe- tence – the coach acting as empowerer will delegate a significant task to a person and offer them support while they carry it out, but will leave the method of carrying it out to the individual concerned; review meetings will tend to focus on how effectively the task was performed and review key learning points that could be valuable in the future. Tom Peters, in *Thriving on Chaos* (1987), introduces the concept of "Failing forward," which means trying things, possibly making mistakes, and learning from them. This is an ideal environment in which to follow this approach (though not in safety-related activities).

The coach may use different methods with the same individual in different aspects of their job. As the individual gains more knowledge, the instructor will tend toward the watching brief, while the guide will tend toward the empowerer.

The coach will be involved very closely with the individual and the regular cycles of:

» identifying needs
» planning to address them
» carrying out the training activities, and
» review

will become part of the performance management process. Formal appraisal sessions will identify specific development needs and set out further development plans.

Mentoring

The main roles of the mentor are to counsel and support. Mentors are usually at a more senior level in the organization than the person whose mentor they will be and are likely to have a more strategic role. The role of mentor requires specific skills that not everyone in the organization might have. It is, therefore, essential for them to be given specific training in how to be one.

Some of the key responsibilities of a mentor might be:

» a guide to further development opportunities;
» a gatekeeper to other key figures in the organization;
» a parental figure with whom to share career aspirations;
» an adviser on the culture of the organization; and
» a supporter during times of stress.

It is important that people meet their mentors on a regular basis. It is also important that both the individual and the mentor know the purpose of the meeting, and an informal agenda is useful.

In those organizations in which mentoring has been found to be ineffective, the failure can usually be put down to either the mentor and/or the individual didn't really understand their roles, or the mentor was not given any guidance upon how to perform the role.

Companies which use mentoring and coaching include Pepsi Cola, Lockheed Martin, and ExxonMobil in the United States.

In fact, ExxonMobil has a very interesting approach to its mentoring system. It:

» pairs up newly hired recruits with experienced professionals, who act as their mentors and help them to understand the company culture and plan their career development; and

» provides new employees with peer support in the form of recently hired people who still remember what it was like when they joined the company and know how the new recruit is feeling. This is often referred to as a "buddy" system.

Coaching and mentoring are important for the future of an organization, because they can help to facilitate the growth and advancement of employees. It is necessary to recognize that, in these days of flatter organizational hierarchies, where the focus is often on team working, there may be fewer opportunities within any one organization for people to advance their careers through promotion.

Coaching allows people to grow within their own jobs and helps them to achieve Maslow's self-actualization, without having to leave the organization for another one.

Mentoring will offer the guidance and support people need to take advantage of any opportunities that do come their way.

METHODS OF TRAINING AND DEVELOPMENT

Earlier in this chapter, we considered the use of individual development plans, which would result in people being able to produce an action plan to address their training and development needs. There is a wide range of learning activities, as we saw in Chapter 2, which might be used by the person to address the training and development needs identified in their action plan.

Table 6.5 identifies the particular value of each method.

Any action plan is likely to have a mix of a variety of methods. One key factor here is the learning style of the person concerned. We saw in Chapter 3 that Honey and Mumford identified four learning styles:

» activists
» reflectors

Table 6.5

Group activities	Particularly useful for:
Action centered	experiencing situations, developing attitudes
Role plays/simulations	applying various skills in a "safe" environment
Presentations	building confidence, developing presentation skills
Case studies	building knowledge, developing analytical skills
Group discussions	exchanging knowledge, testing out ideas
Learning support groups	offering mutual support, developing attitudes
Lectures	disseminating information to a lot of people
Video	showing good practice versus poor practice
One to one	
Mentoring	providing guidance and support to individuals
Coaching	developing knowledge, skills, and attitudes through individual action plans
Individual work	
Individual research	building knowledge
Work assignments	testing knowledge and application of skills
Practice	building confidence and competence
Internet	building knowledge and skills
Tapes	reinforcing learning
CD-ROM	interactive learning
Organizational	
Job shadowing	building new skills and new perspectives
Attachments	practicing new skills and seeing new perspectives
Job swaps	practicing new skills and seeing new perspectives
Networking	exchanging ideas, developing contacts
Company intranet	building knowledge, skills, and attitudes

» theorists
» pragmatists.

If possible, the methods used should appeal to the person's preferred style because they are more likely to benefit from it. For example, activists, who like to "do things," will learn a lot from action-centered learning, but are likely to be particularly bored by a lecture. Similarly, reflectors, who prefer to observe other people "doing things," may learn less from being involved in a role play and more from the reflection and analysis that follows it. You can find out more about learning styles in Chapter 8.

EVALUATION: CHICKEN OR EGG?

Many organizations find evaluating the benefits of their training and development activities very difficult. This is often because they leave the evaluation until the end, when, in fact, it should be considered at the very beginning.

But how can you evaluate, if you don't know what you are trying to achieve in the first place?

Earlier in this chapter, and also in Chapter 2, we saw the value of carrying out a training needs analysis. This allows us to identify any training and development gaps, and the purpose of the training is to close those gaps.

If we know exactly what the gap is, we can know when we have closed it; we can, therefore, set out some clear, specific, and measurable training and development objectives. At the same time as we establish the objectives, we need to work out how we establish that we have achieved them. We can identify the following stages in the process.

» Analyze levels of knowledge, skills, and attitudes required.
» Identify current levels.
» Establish gap.
» Set objectives.
» Decide evaluation method.
» Deliver training.
» Evaluate.

Clearly, evaluation is both chicken and egg!

We can look at an example. An organization has established that its sales team is not hitting its targets. It appears that some people are making a lot of appointments with customers, but are failing to turn many of these opportunities into sales. A training needs analysis suggests that they are failing to listen clearly to what the customer is saying.

The training gap has been established. We now need to work out what we actually want to achieve in measurable terms. We want to improve the listening skills of the staff concerned and we can express this in several ways as shown in Table 6.6.

Table 6.6

Objective	Evaluated by:
If there is a specific course available which provides certificates for people who pass it successfully, we might agree an objective that everyone concerned achieves a minimum of a merit (better than average) pass	checking the certificate at the end of the course. This does not necessarily prove that people can transfer this success to the workplace
If they have already agreed a rating for the skill with their manager of, say, 5 out of 10, they could agree a target of reaching 8 out of 10 within two months	the manager observing the person either in a real appointment or in a role play
Or, we could look at the ratio of appointments to sales. If a sale is currently made in one of every eight appointments, we could agree an objective of increasing that to one in every six within two months and to one in every three within six months	keeping a record of the ratio over a period of time to see whether the required improvements have occurred. This should eventually feed through into improved sales results

The weakness of the first of the evaluation methods shown above is that it does not measure actual improvements in the workplace.

The second method allows a person to demonstrate the value of the training in a real situation.

The particular value of the third method is that it specifically links the effectiveness of the training to the organization's bottom line. The organization can work out what it has spent on training and how much its sales results have improved because of it. It can, therefore, see the return on its investment.

We will look at evaluation again in Chapters 8 and 10.

EDUCATING THE CUSTOMER

Many organizations recognize the part that customers play in the success of their products.

Many service organizations, for example, require customers to be involved at the point where the service is delivered. Hotels need to ensure that their customers can evacuate the building in case of emergency. Manufacturers need customers to use their products in the correct way.

This involvement is becoming even more pronounced with the arrival of e-commerce because the customer often has the technology to link directly into the organization's operating systems and may even perform some of the tasks themselves.

Here are just two of the many examples of organizations which recognize that there may be a need for customer training as well as employee training.

The UK financial services company Egg offers tools for customers to practice on before decisions are made. These include the "Investor Profiler" and the "Virtual Portfolio" where a customer can build a pretend portfolio of shares and investment funds and watch what happens to their investment.

American Airlines have installed, in cooperation with the Federal Air Administration, a number of "Know before you go" kiosks at a number of airports in the United States to educate customers as to what can be taken onto an airplane and what cannot.

KEY LEARNING POINTS
» Training and development can play a key role in times of major change.

» Traditional and open learning methods can both play a significant role.
» There has been a change from focusing on the inputs of training to focusing on the outputs.
» Coaches and mentors can play valuable roles.
» There are a variety of training and development methods, each with their own advantages in particular situations.
» Evaluation of training and development has never been more important.
» The training and development of customers who take part in the company's operations must not be overlooked.

Success Stories

This chapter includes case studies of:

» American Airlines
» Financial Services National Training Organization (FS NTO), UK
» Commonwealth Bank of Australia
» National Air Traffic Services Ltd.

We can look in more detail at some very successful organizations who are putting into practice the concepts of training and development. The four organizations we will be looking are as follows.

» **Commonwealth Bank of Australia** - a commercial bank with a world-wide presence.
» **American Airlines** - a commercial global airline, based in the United States, but with code sharing facilities with British Airways and part of the Oneworld Alliance.
» **The Financial Services National Training Organization (FS NTO)** - an organization, operating in the UK, which exists to support companies in the financial services industry to improve the quality and skills of their employees.
» **National Air Traffic Services Ltd** - a UK organization which exists to ensure that air traffic is moved safely and expeditiously, and which is currently in the process of moving into a public–private partnership.

Each case study has a different focus and will give us the opportunity of exploring different aspects of training and development.

» The case study of Commonwealth Bank of Australia looks at a company which applies all of the approaches that we would expect in a major organization.
» The case study of American Airlines presents some of the more unusual initiatives that this innovative company has implemented.
» The case study of the FS NTO looks at a whole industry that is changing culture through a training and competency framework.
» The case study of National Air Traffic Services Ltd considers a specific example of a successful long-running development program.

CASE STUDY: COMMONWEALTH BANK OF AUSTRALIA

The privatization of the Commonwealth Bank Group was completed in 1997 and, since then, it has grown to be one of the largest in Australia and one of the top hundred in the world. It has over 9 million customers and some 37,000 staff. It provides a wide range of financial services, including banking, insurance, and fund management. Due to its expansion after privatization, it has a world-wide presence and is represented in the following countries:

» New Zealand
» People's Republic of China
» Fiji
» Japan
» Hong Kong
» Thailand
» Vietnam
» Indonesia
» the UK
» Malaysia
» the Philippines
» Singapore
» the United States.

The bank has a very innovative approach and has joint ventures with organizations such as McDonald's, Vodafone, and Woolworths.

The scene for the bank's training and development effort is set by its advert to attract graduates to join the company. It speaks of wanting people with a "passion for knowledge and a strong desire to succeed."

It promises, in return, to "provide challenges and rewards in a career development program designed to help them to achieve their goals and aspirations."

It goes on to promise in-depth training and ongoing development opportunities, with people acquiring new skills and refining existing skills. It offers the opportunity to follow a career path, with full support of the company's resources, expertise, and knowledge.

In this case study, we can look at the following programs:

» graduate employees
» branch customer service officers.

Graduate programs

Graduate programs aimed at fast tracking graduates into senior positions operate in the following business units:

» Customer Services
» Australian Financial Services
» Institutional Banking
» Technology, Operations, and Property
» Financial and Risk Management
» Group Human Resources.

Each program differs slightly because it is tailored to the needs of the particular business unit. For example:

» Group Human Resources stresses the variety of challenging roles which will allow people to develop their skills.
» Customer Services stresses the Australia-wide placements, with a senior manager as mentor.
» Technology, Operations. and Property offers exposure to key strategic initiatives, working as part of a project team. Other learning opportunities include workshops, site visits, and coaching.

What is common with all of them is that there are a variety of challenging opportunities which allow people to develop and grow. Another common factor is that the management of the individual's career is their own responsibility rather than the company's, though they are offered every resource to assist them to plan it.

The company also has a program in which it invites a limited number of undergraduates, who are in their second-last year, to work with them during their summer vacation. This helps the students to learn about business before they leave university and allows them to gain some knowledge of the company's culture and procedures.

Customer service officers

Customer service officers are based in branches and carry out the following activities:

» answer customer inquiries;
» talk to them about their financial needs;
» tell them about the services and products available; and
» refer them to specialist financial advisers.

Everyone is given an orientation program to acquaint them with the company.

Training is then provided both on and off the job to enable them to build up their skills in the areas of:

» sales techniques
» customer service
» products and services
» questioning techniques
» listening skills
» systems and procedures.

The training consists of the following methods:

» off-site training courses;
» coaching on the job;
» self-paced learning; and
» in-house short training sessions.

The company also has its own internal TV service, Commonwealth Bank of Australia TV, which is also used for training purposes.

Clearly, then, we can see that the company uses the whole range of training and development resources available to help its staff to grow.

Time line

» **1911** Created by Act of Parliament
» **1959** Central bank functions moved to Reserve Bank of Australia
» **1989** Purchased 75% of ASB Bank Ltd of New Zealand
» **1991** Became a public company, 30% of shares offered for sale
» **1993** Commonwealth government sold more shares, retaining 50.4%
» **1996** Commonwealth government sold the rest of its shares
» **1997** Privatization finalized, expansion begun nationally and overseas
» **2000** Purchased the remainder of ASB
» **2000** Purchased Colonial Limited, a life insurance, banking, and funds management group, making the Commonwealth Bank Group a fully integrated financial services business.

KEY INSIGHTS

» Various types of entry into the company depending upon career aspirations.
» Use of mentors.
» Use of coaching.
» Attachments.
» Work assignments (projects).
» Working in teams.
» Use of workshops to support learning.

Let's now look at American Airlines, to see some of its interesting approaches to training and development, some of which are very innovative.

CASE STUDY: AMERICAN AIRLINES

In this case study, we can look at some of the specific initiatives being pursued by the airline. It is owned by the holding company AMR Corp. and consists of:

» American Airlines (Passenger and Cargo Divisions)
» American Eagle Airlines
» AMR Investment Services.

In April 2001, with the purchase of the airline TWA, American Airlines became the largest airline in the world. Don Carty, however, the company's chief executive, says, "that was never our goal. We've set a course to be the greatest airline in the world ... and we plan to do that by achieving leadership in Safety, Product, Network, Technology, Service and Culture. Being the largest airline in the world is not a bad side benefit, but being the best should be our one and only goal."

In conjunction with its various partners (it is part of the Oneworld Alliance) the company can move passengers and cargo to most parts of the world and can certainly be described as a global company. Air travel is a very competitive environment and airlines need to recruit and develop high-caliber individuals throughout a variety of disciplines.

Here are a few of the innovative initiatives that American Airlines, in addition to its standard methods of training and development, has adopted over the last few years in its drive toward being "the best:"

» flagship university
» career opportunity system
» home computer packages
» CR Smith Museum
» life balance
» environmental training
» customer education kiosks.

Flagship university

The university's main base is located in a large training and conference center in Fort Worth, Texas. The flagship team constantly designs new ways of delivering education, training, and development opportunities to the company's employees. The aim is to allow them to grow, both professionally and personally. It produces its own training videos, computer-based training packages, and Web-based training.

The university has continued to expand its programs which now cover:

» management
» supervisors
» customer services
» flight services
» reservations
» cargo
» ramp services
» regulated training (e.g. safety).

There are over 60 programs available for personal and professional development, delivered by experienced company employees with extensive training experience.

Career opportunity system

American Airlines has a user-friendly, interactive Web-based career opportunity system. It allows managers who have vacancies in their departments to post them on the system, access candidate lists, and research the candidates' qualifications. It also allows them to approve applicants from their own department who are seeking advertised vacancies.

Job candidates can search through vacancies on the system for all levels of jobs up to middle management. They can also create their resume online.

The system makes it much easier for them to find new challenges within the company and makes it less likely that they will look outside, taking their valuable skills elsewhere.

Home computer packages

We saw, in our case study in Chapter 4, that the UK-based company PowerGen is providing its employees with home computer packages at a very low subsidized price. In the year 2000, in order to give its employees the opportunity to develop themselves further, American Airlines offered them a comprehensive package, called On Time, On Line, including a personal computer, monitor, printer, Internet access, and in-home repair. Employees will be able to access the company intranet for all the company information they need.

CR Smith Museum

The CR Smith Museum is located in Fort Worth, Texas, and focuses totally on commercial aviation. It was opened in 1993 and is dedicated to past and present American Airlines employees and, in particular, to C.R. Smith, the aviation pioneer who was the company's long-time president.

Its aim is education through enjoyment. It provides a family experience in which the world of flight can be seen, heard, and touched. It is run on a non-profit basis by the CR Smith Aviation Museum Foundation. It is funded through gifts from corporate partners, current company employees, retired employees, and friends of the museum.

Since 1994, the museum has hosted its Eagle Aviation Academy, a five-day intensive introduction to aviation for young people in the fifth to eighth grades. It offers them the opportunity to consider careers in aviation. The course, for which a fee is charged, allows them to develop an interest in the role of aviation in history. It also introduces them to some of the basic concepts of flight, through hands-on workstations and special projects. There are also field trips to American Airlines facilities and other aviation-related points of interest.

Life balance

When Don Carty took over as chief executive in 1998, he immediately began to address the issue of the company's corporate culture. The balance of home and work was a particular concern to him and a work/life department was set up to provide employees with a resource where they could access help on a wide range of personal issues.

The aim is to equip employees with a variety of tools to help them manage the various commitments and challenges in their personal and professional lives, recognizing their responsibilities to their work, their homes and families, their community, and to themselves.

Underlying this initiative is the company belief that "motivated and engaged employees deliver the quality of service and personal attention, which in turn creates satisfied customers whose repeat business naturally rewards shareholders."

The company is particularly concerned about the future, and there-fore about children, because they are the future. The company aims to demonstrate that it cares about:

» its employees' children – which it shows through the LifeBalance program, summer jobs for the children, and the home computer packages mentioned above;
» children throughout the community – which it shows by becoming involved in a variety of schemes to improve the lives of children throughout the world; and
» future employees – which is shown through the many educational projects that it supports, such as the summer schools at the CR Smith Museum.

Environmental training

The company has a four-day course in environmental training, which, after detailed scrutiny of its curriculum, has just been awarded certification by the National Environmental Training Association (NETA).

The course is needed for some 1000 environmental coordinators at the company's facilities around the world. It was set up a decade ago as part of a drive to increase the number of coordinators at the company's numerous airport locations. Its aim is to produce safety in the workplace and compliance with regulatory safety requirements.

Tim Ahern, the vice-president of safety, security, and environment, says that the company is "honored to have an environmental organization such as NETA recognize our training efforts. It demonstrates to our employees, our customers, and the communities we serve, that American is committed to environmental stewardship."

NETA, founded in 1977 with the support of the US Environment and Protection Agency, is an international non-profit-making educational and professional society dedicated to promoting competency and excellence in environmental health and safety training.

Customer education kiosks

Finally, we can look at an example of how American Airlines trains its customers. Customers are an important part of any operation and, as we saw in Chapter 6, they may need to be trained in order to play their part fully and safely. This is particularly relevant to the airline industry.

American Airlines and the Federal Aviation Administration (FAA) have long recognized the importance of ensuring that people understand the restrictions on carrying dangerous goods and hazardous materials on-board planes.

American Airlines, American Eagle Airlines, and the FAA have joined forces to produce customer education kiosks at a number of airports, including Miami, Kennedy, and La Guardia in New York, Chicago, Boston, San Jose, and San Juan, and there are several more to follow.

There are similar kiosks in several of the company's cargo facilities too.

Under this program, identified as "know before you go," customers can have their questions answered about what can be packed where and what must not be taken on-board at all.

Time line

» **1992** AMR Consulting Group formed to take advantage of growing demand for services in airline-related businesses
» **1993** (July) AMR expanded to become AMR Training and Consulting Group
» **1993** CR Smith Museum opened
» **1994** Eagle Aviation Academy introduced
» **1998** Don Carty becomes chief executive
» **1998** LifeBalance program introduced
» **1999** (February) Oneworld Alliance begins
» **1999** (March) American Eagle Airlines acquired Business Express Airlines
» **2000** (December) Business Express Airlines fully integrated into American Eagle Airlines
» **2000** Computer packages offered to employees
» **2000** Flagship university launched
» **2000** Roll-out of hazardous goods kiosks
» **2001** (April) Purchase of the airline TWA is completed and American Airlines becomes the largest airline in the world
» **2001** Environmental training course certified by NETA.

KEY INSIGHTS
» The use of a variety of approaches to training and development.
» The importance of innovation.
» The use of new technology.
» The importance of valuing people.
» The link between motivation and growth.
» Investing in the future workforce.
» Offering people a variety of challenges.
» Simplifying the advancement system.
» Recognizing the need to grow both at work and at home.

We can now look at the third case study in this chapter, which will show how a whole industry can be involved in a specific approach to training and development.

CASE STUDY: THE FINANCIAL SERVICES NATIONAL TRAINING ORGANIZATION

In this case study we will be looking at the financial services industry in the UK. Let's first establish the background.

Background

Because of the financial services industry's key role both in terms of the wider economy and in providing financial advice to help people to manage their individual finances, the industry has a regulator to oversee its activities and ensure that customers receive the best possible advice. All organizations in the industry must comply with any requirements set out by this regulator.

In 1995, the then regulator, the Personal Investment Authority (PIA), set out some guiding principles, which covered training and competency of financial advisers (and of people supervising financial advisers) and was known as the PIA Training and Competency Scheme.

This document was very prescriptive of the types of training and development that had to be carried out and required organizations to take a training and competency approach. It also required them to have a person specifically responsible for training and competency, who was referred to as the training and competency officer.

The scheme focused mainly on the inputs to training, for example suggesting that advisers must carry out at least 50 hours of continued professional development. It did not focus on the application of the learning resulting from that development, nor did it take account of the fact that different people might learn at different speeds, so 50 hours of development might be quite adequate for one person and totally inadequate for another.

In 1997 the Financial Services Authority (FSA) was established to become the main regulator of the industry and it has been working in parallel with the PIA to produce a new Training and Competency Scheme which focuses more on the outputs of training and development rather than the inputs. A consultation document was sent out to the industry in the year 2000 and the scheme is due to be introduced in November 2001.

The key aims of the FSA are to:

» maintain confidence in the UK financial system;
» promote public understanding of the financial system;
» build a clear framework of standards in the UK and internationally;
» secure an appropriate degree of protection for consumers; and
» contribute to the reduction of financial crime.

In the new scheme, it recognizes:

» the responsibilities that a company's own management has to ensure that its staff are fully competent to practice their profession;
» the need for a company to be efficient in the use of its resources; and
» the need to balance the restrictions placed on a company with the benefits of regulation for consumers.

To this end, it has become far less prescriptive and focuses more on the minimum standards of competence that people must demonstrate, rather than setting out how individuals should be trained. It leaves the decision about how to ensure that competence is achieved to the individual organization itself, giving it the flexibility that it did not have under the previous scheme.

The key measures of effective training and development are now related to how people behave, the levels of knowledge they demonstrate, and the satisfaction felt by their customers.

It was also recognized that there were varying levels of understanding of how to build up competence in the industry ranging from the very large company, employing hundreds of financial advisers, with its own specialist trainers and coaches and its own training departments to ensure best practice is observed, to the much smaller company with only a few individuals who might have more limited access to training and development opportunities.

Because of this, and because of the move away from being prescriptive, the FSA felt that some guidance would be necessary for many organizations in the industry, especially the smaller ones which would not have established training and development systems like the larger firms, including many independent financial advisers (IFAs). It, therefore, encouraged the industry to develop "toolkits" to help itself by setting standards of best practice.

This is where the Financial Services National Training Organization took the initiative, supported by a number of institutes and trade bodies within the industry.

Financial Services National Training Organization (FS NTO)

The FS NTO's mission is to "support employers and work in partnership to improve the quality and skills of the workforce as a fundamental requirement for the sustainable competitiveness of the industry."

Its key aims are focused around:

» promoting learning in the industry;
» striving for the highest standards of competence;
» sharing knowledge with the industry;
» influencing training initiatives; and
» looking toward the skills needed in the future.

The FS NTO decided to produce various toolkits, which would give guidance and demonstrate best practice in training and development for specific sectors of the industry. The toolkit would be available both in hard copy and in electronic form; it would be free to members of the supporting institutes and trade bodies, with a small charge being made for others.

The toolkit is a set of resources which includes:

» accepted industry standards
» practical examples of procedures and documentation
» best practice case studies
» the latest educational models and thinking.

The FS NTO came into being in March 2001, as part of the amalgamation of the formerly separate Banking and Insurance NTOs. Each of the latter had already begun to work toward producing toolkits for various aspects of the profession, so, for example, there was a "Banking" toolkit and a "Financial Adviser" toolkit as well as several others.

Here, we can look in more detail at one particular toolkit, which covers the training and development of the financial adviser. It became available in June 2001.

Financial adviser's toolkit

The toolkit aims to set out best practice for financial advisers, so that everyone who uses it will be aware of what standards they should be aiming for and what systems and processes they can use to achieve those standards.

The toolkit for financial advisers covers the following areas:

» FSA Training and Competence Policy
» FSA Training and Competence Framework
» Assessment
» Training and development
» Managing advisers
» Recruitment.

FSA Training and Competence Policy

This sets out the culture and policies and stresses the move away from training inputs and toward training outputs.

FSA Training and Competence Framework

This identifies the various stages that an adviser must go through in order to gain full competence, setting out the levels of activity that can and cannot be carried out during each stage. It also identifies the main areas of knowledge, skills, and attitudes that a competent financial adviser should demonstrate.

It identifies six main areas of competence:

» client interaction
» administration
» business quality
» business production
» being a team player
» developing your own competence.

Each of these areas have their own specific knowledge, skills, and attitudes. For example, for successful interaction with clients, the adviser will need:

» knowledge – such as financial qualifications, knowledge of the company's products
» skills – such as advisory skills, data gathering skills
» attitudes – having a passion for delivering excellent service.

Assessment

Clearly, where people have to be competent before they can practice their profession, there have to be formal assessments. The toolkit covers the whole range of options that are available and looks at the situations in which they might be applied. It also considers the vital aspect of maintaining clear records and documentation.

Training and development

The toolkit contains the whole spectrum of training and development methods, and identifies which will be most effective for particular situations and for individual advisers. It suggests individual training plans for each adviser like those we mentioned in Chapter 6. It covers all aspects of training and development, including orientation, which we met in Chapter 2.

The change in the regulator's policy from focusing on inputs to focusing on outputs means that an organization can choose which training methods it is most comfortable with, as long as it produces competent people as an end result.

Managing advisers

Managers spend a lot of time working one to one with advisers and the toolkit identifies the skills they will need in coaching and assessment

Recruitment

The toolkit recognizes that, before any recruitment can be carried out, the organization must have a clear idea of the areas of competence needed by its staff. Only then can it ensure that it has selected the right individuals who will benefit from the development program and who will progress through to fully competent adviser status.

In addition to the toolkits themselves, the FS NTO has also set up a series of workshops both to promote their use and to explain the advantages that using them will bring, especially to those organizations who have not had any great experience in setting up these types of framework.

Research

In addition to the above, a lot of research went into the production of the toolkit, as it contains a large number of documents and procedures. These were volunteered by those organizations which already have excellent systems up and running and it is a good example of competitor organizations being prepared to help others within the industry in the interests of raising the standards of the industry as a whole.

We saw this earlier, in Chapter 5, in the airline industry and it is an excellent feature of industries which put the security (whether safety or financial) of the customer first.

Of course, the focus of the most successful companies will be on training and developing their advisers to give their customers the very best, impartial advice, which will, almost by definition, satisfy its regulatory requirements.

Time line

- » **1995**: PIA Training and Competency Scheme introduced
- » **1997**: Financial Services Authority (FSA) set up in parallel to the PIA
- » **2000**: FSA consults the industry on a new Training and Competency Scheme
- » **2000**: Toolkits developed, supported by several institutes and trade bodies
- » **2001**: (March) Formation of a new Financial Services NTO
- » **2001**: (June) Financial advisers toolkit made available
- » **2001**: (June onwards) Toolkit workshops program
- » **2001**: (November) FSA Training and Competency Scheme introduced.

KEY INSIGHTS

- » National training organizations can play a significant part in guiding their industry.

> » A whole industry can be influenced by its approach to training and development.
> » Smaller companies may need the help of best practice toolkits.
> » Competitors can cooperate for the benefit of the customer, especially in regulated industries where there are safety or financial implications.
> » Training and competency frameworks allow an organization to be confident that it is meeting its customers' and, where applicable, its regulator's requirements.
> » The focus on outputs allows an organization to focus on the benefits that result from training.

Let's now consider our final case study in this chapter and take a look at the Certificate in Management program that has been running for several years at National Air Traffic Services Ltd. It has been taking place against a background of very significant change for the organization.

CASE STUDY: NATIONAL AIR TRAFFIC SERVICES LTD (NATS)

NATS is responsible for ensuring that air traffic is moved both safely and expeditiously around the UK and over the North Atlantic Ocean. It is currently undergoing a significant period of change, both in the way it carries out its operations and to its funding and structure.

The company currently handles around 2 million flights per year; its operations cover "en route" traffic through UK airspace, and it controls some 14 airports around the UK, including the largest ones at Heathrow, Gatwick, Stansted, Birmingham, Manchester, and Glasgow.

"En route" services are currently handled by three centers at West Drayton, near Heathrow, Prestwick, in Ayshire, Scotland, and Manchester. In the future, all "en route" services will be handled by two centers, namely the almost completed new center at Swanwick, in Hampshire, and the completely new center that will be built at Prestwick.

In addition to these major operational changes, the organization, itself, has been prepared, over the past decade, to move from the public into the private sector. In 1994, the government announced that it intended to privatize the company, which was then one business within the CAA, which also looked after the safety and economic regulation of air travel.

In order to distance NATS, the service provider of air traffic control, from the regulatory side of the CAA, in 1996 NATS became a wholly owned subsidiary of the CAA. The result of this was that some shared services were separated out and NATS had to provide for its own future.

In 1999, it was announced that a public–private partnership would go ahead and bidders to be the strategic partner were invited. In March 2001, the Airline Group, formed by an alliance of several airlines, was announced as the new partner. They would have some 46% of shares, with the government retaining 49% and the staff having 5%. The partnership was officially implemented in July 2001.

So, clearly, the organization has moved from being very much a governmental organization to be at least partly in the private sector within the last five years. Such a change demanded a significant change in organizational culture, which has been achieved in various ways, not least through a significant investment in training for its managers.

In 1993, the CAA, as a whole, decided to introduce a rolling program for its managers and potential managers which would lead to them being awarded a Certificate in Management Studies (CMS), an internationally recognized managerial qualification. NATS was much the largest part of the CAA and it, therefore, had the largest number of people undergoing the program.

There was a twofold strategy:

» to improve the management skills of its employees; and
» to move toward a more customer-focused culture.

The program was provided by a consortium consisting of a training company and a university. It was more of a development program looking to extend the skills levels of the learners rather than a training program.

The course itself consisted of several modules covering:

» leadership
» team work
» finance

- » problem solving
- » motivation
- » business environment
- » communication
- » performance
- » marketing
- » customer service
- » operations
- » managing change.

These were chosen because they fitted both the organization's competency framework and the university's academic syllabus.

The program was based on the open learning model, supported by workshops and a residential weekend. The methods used on the year-long program included the following.

- » An introductory workshop.
- » A set of interactive workbooks covering the above topics.
- » A series of workshops, supporting the workbooks, in which skills could be practiced in a safe environment. Typically, these would consist of group exercises, discussions, case studies, and presentations.
- » A three-day residential workshop, which allowed learners to practice a number of skills from a variety of different topics; typically it would consist of an extended role play in which groups would have to apply a wide range of skills combining marketing, operations, finance, and team working.
- » Written assignments were submitted on each topic, with a more substantial assignment at the end of the program which again allowed learners to demonstrate skills across different topics.
- » A tutor available for advice, who also assessed the assignments.

The aim of the program was to introduce people to some of the managerial theories and then enable them to practice their new skills in their own workplace with their own teams. The program is a very successful one and is still continuing, and is updated every couple of years.

To date, several hundred managers have gained their certificates and the program is seen as a great success. Graduates of the course are presented with their certificates at a ceremony, usually hosted by the chief executive.

Apart from the numbers of managers achieving their certificates, evaluation of the success of the program can be measured on the following levels, that we identified in Chapter 3.

» **Reaction** – how do people feel during and immediately after the training?
  » Feedback forms at each event
  » Feedback forms in each workbook.
» **Learning** – how much have they learned in terms of knowledge skills and attitudes?
  » Pre-course skills benchmarking questionnaires, compared to post-course questionnaires
  » Feedback from colleagues and their team.
» **Performance** – what are they now doing differently as a result of the learning experience?
  » Feedback from separate section in the final extended assignment, detailing what they are doing differently as a result of the program.
» **Organizational results** – what additional benefits has the organization gained?
  » Individuals began to be more effective and achieved improved results against their key objectives
  » Many managers now have the CMS.
» **Ultimate value** – has the training helped the organization meets its strategic mission and goals, in terms of profitability, growth, or survival?
  » Helped to move it toward a more customer-focused approach.

Following the success of the CMS program, a Diploma in Management Studies (DMS) was introduced, operating in a similar way, in 1995. The following time line outlines the key changes that were taking place during the program.

Time line

» **1990**: Monopoly and Merger's Commission calls for the separation of air traffic service provision from regulation

» **1991**: Work starts on the new air traffic control center at Swanwick, Hampshire
» **1993**: First CMS program introduced
» **1994**: The intention to privatize NATS is announced
» **1995**: DMS introduced
» **1996**: NATS becomes a wholly owned subsidiary of the Civil Aviation Authority
» **1997**: The government announces that it wants a public–private partnership (PPP) for NATS
» **1998**: First major revision of the CMS program, rebranded as a NATS rather than a CAA program
» **1999**: Bill leading to PPP introduced to parliament
» **2001**: Second major revision of the CMS program
» **2001**: Airline Group announced as the new strategic partner under PPP
» **2001**: NATS/Airline Group partnership implemented
» **2002**: Expected opening of the new center at Swanwick.

KEY INSIGHTS

» Open learning approach is employed successfully.
» A variety of developmental methods were used.
» Success of the program is apparent at all evaluation levels.
» Program helped to change the organizational culture.
» A variety of skills were both learned and practiced.
» The content of the course was tailored to align with the organization's competency framework.
» The program allowed networking between people in different departments.
» There was group development as well as individual development.
» People were more prepared to handle the change process.

Key Concepts and Thinkers

Training and development have a very wide range of concepts. This chapter includes a glossary of the terms that are used. It includes:

» explanations of the most common terms
» key writers and thinkers.

Training and development have a very wide range of concepts. This chapter includes a glossary of the terms that are used, covering both explanations of the most common terms and key concepts and thinkers

GLOSSARY

Action-centered learning – usually involves a task or series of tasks carried out by a group. It can be relatively short, taking place over a couple of hours, or more extended, taking a weekend or even a week. Typically, the members of the group will face challenging tasks which they help each other to carry out and reflect back on the key learning points at regular intervals. They apply the lessons learned to the next part of the task. All aspects of the learning cycle can be experienced and group development can take place.

Attachments – (or secondments) being attached to a particular section or unit that is not your own usual place of work. Typically, attachments will last two months or more and will give the person an opportunity to see the organization from a different perspective and to develop additional skills.

Behaviorism – the theory that suggests that people's behavior can be influenced through rewards and punishments.

Case studies – written examples of events that have happened (they could be fictional) which people can analyze, then find solutions to problems, or identify courses of action. Learning points are then applied to the person's own work situation.

Coaching – working with an individual, usually on a one-to-one basis; the topic is covered in detail in Chapter 6.

Cognitive theory – the theory that people do not simply respond to stimuli, but process information in the brain before responding.

Competence – the knowledge, skills, and attitudes that are needed to carry out a particular task.

Competent – being able to satisfy the requirements of knowledge, skills, and attitudes that are needed to carry out a particular task.

Conditioning – there are two main types:

» classic (or response) conditioning, which suggests that we respond in a particular way to either positive or negative stimuli; and

» operant conditioning, which examines how different behaviors can be established by reinforcing them with rewards.

Development – preparing for the next role (or even the one after that), whether moving to a new job or taking on additional tasks or responsibilities in one's current job.

Evaluation – judging how effective the training and development have been. It is covered in more detail in Chapter 6.

Feedback – giving people information about their performance. There are two main types:

» motivational, which is used to comment on good performance and helps to build a person's confidence; and

» developmental, which is used to improve performance and helps to build a person's competence.

Group discussion – several people discuss a topic and exchange ideas on it. They identify the key learning points and apply them to their own jobs It is a very useful tool for group learning as it encourages synergy and often produces innovative ideas. It is good for team building too.

Individual research – involves a person seeking information and working on their own. It may involve reading books, magazines, searching the Internet, and carrying out interviews.

Internet – the World Wide Web which offers access to a huge store of information and also to a large number of training packages.

Intranet – a more limited version of the Internet, usually set up within an organization and providing access only to the employees of the organization.

Job shadowing – observing someone doing their job in order to learn new skills and see new perspectives. It is a particularly good idea if it is to be the person's next job.

Job swaps – exchanging jobs with someone to develop new skills and see new perspectives.

Learner – anyone who is prepared to learn.

Learning cycle – was identified by Kolb *et al*. and sets out the four elements of the learning process:

» having an experience;

» reflecting on it;

» forming abstract concepts and generalizations; and

» testing the implications of these concepts in different situations.

They repeat themselves in a continuous cycle.

Learning styles – were identified by Honey and Mumford and are linked to the learning cycle. They are covered in more detail later in this chapter.

Learning support groups – formal or informal networks of people who support each other through the learning process. They are often set up in open learning programs, so that people can keep in touch and exchange ideas.

Lecture – one (or more) person disseminating information to a group of people. It tends to consist largely of one-way communication, though it can be useful when information has to be passed to a large number of people.

Mentor – a senior member of the organization who provides guidance and support to people.

Networking – meeting people from a variety of areas within (or outside) the organization. Developing informal relationships in this way widens a person's perspective on the organization. They will also be able to put names to faces, which is always useful and helps to facilitate future transactions.

Neuro-linguistic programming (NLP) – a new approach to learning, which is covered later in this chapter.

Objectives – should set out what the organization hopes to achieve with its training and development activities. They should be SMART:
» Specific
» Measurable
» Agreed
» Realistic
» Time bound.

Program – a series of training activities woven together for a specific purpose. A graduate management program, for example, may last 18 months to two years and consist of a number of different modules and learning opportunities.

Role plays/simulations – simulate real-life situations and allow people to apply skills, knowledge, and attitudes to situations that are likely to occur in their jobs. Essentially, they provide a safe environment in which to develop skills and gain confidence. They are particularly useful for practicing the following.

» Situations which happen less often in real life, as the individual has the opportunity to practice in between the events happening for real.

» Emergency situations, where training in the real situation would be too late. Airline simulators are good examples of these. Military exercises and emergency fire and accident drills are also good examples.

» Unpleasant situations, such as dealing with violent or angry customers.

Self-development – taking responsibility for one's own learning and growth. This is covered in more detail later in this chapter.

Team roles – identified by Professor Meredith Belbin. There are nine natural team roles that are needed in any team. This topic is covered in more detail later in this chapter.

Training – gaining the knowledge, skills, and attitudes to carry out the current job.

Training gap – the gap between the levels of knowledge, skills, and attitudes that a person needs to do their job and the levels they are currently displaying.

Training needs analysis – the process of:

» analyzing what knowledge, skills, and attitudes are needed;

» analyzing the levels that are being displayed currently;

» establishing the gap between them; and

» setting out strategies for closing the gap.

Tutor – a person who delivers learning opportunities for people. This can be on a one-to-one basis or in a group. The tutor may facilitate learning or actually teach or instruct. They will usually be able to provide support and knowledge and often act as a resource through a help line or e-mail.

Work assignments – pieces of work, which can be:

» written;

» presented; or

» project managed.

They are useful in enabling an individual to demonstrate their understanding of a particular activity or set of activities.

Let's now focus on a few of the key concepts and thinkers.

KEY CONCEPTS AND THINKERS

Katherine Briggs, Isabel Briggs-Myers, and David Keirsey

Katherine Briggs and Isabel Briggs-Meyers developed a test to identify a person's preferred way of working and interacting with others. The test, usually referred to as the MBTI test (Myers Briggs Type Indicator), first analyzes how people:

» gather information – either by sensing (S) or intuition (N); and
» make decisions – either by thinking (T) or feeling (F).

People gather information either by:

» sensing – systematically gathering hard, measurable data; or by
» intuition – using insight, imagination, or gut feeling.

People make decisions either by:

» thinking – using logical analysis; or by
» feeling – relying on their own beliefs and experience.

This gives four different types of ways in which they gather information and make decisions.

» Intuitive thinking (NT) – uses imagination, though proceeds in a logical way.
» Intuitive feeling (NF) – uses own imagination and values.
» Sensing thinking (ST) – analyses hard data in a logical methodical way.
» Sensing feeling (SF) – uses hard data, but modified by own values.

These types are further modified by how they:

» relate to other people – either extrovert (E) or introvert (I); and
» allocate priorities – either judgmental (J) or perceptive (P).

People relate to other people either as:

» introverts – who may prefer to be alone; or as
» extroverts – who thrive in the company of other people.

When people allocate priorities, they are either:

» judgmental - making a rational judgment on the order of priorities; or
» perceptive - tending to be more spontaneous.

When these extra dimensions are applied to the four types mentioned above, the result is 16 types. The Myers-Briggs approach suggests that, once a person is identified as a particular type, their behaviors in certain situations can be predicted. This has significant implications for managers and for their future development.

There are a number of interpretations of the behaviors that each of the 16 types will display. David Keirsey's is one of the best known and he uses the labels shown in Fig. 8.1.

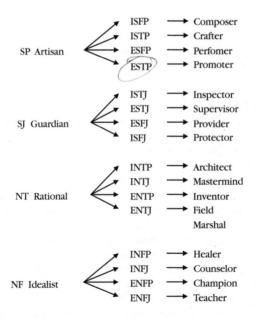

Fig. 8.1

A full description of each type can be found on David Keirsey's Temperament Sorter; the Website address is www.keirsey.com.

There are many companies who offer to carry out the MBTI test for individuals or organizations.

Highlights

Books:

Briggs-Myers, I. & McCaulley, M.H. (1985) *Manual: A Guide to the Development and Use of the Myers Briggs Type Indicator*. Consulting Psychologists Press, Palo Alto, CA.

Briggs-Myers, I. & Myers, P. (1980) *Gifts Differing*. Consulting Psychologists Press, Palo Alto, CA.

Keirsey D. & Bates, M. (1984) *Please Understand Me: Character and Temperament Types*. Prometheus Nemesis, Del Mar, CA.

Keirsey, D. (1987) *Portraits of Temperament*. Prometheus Nemesis, Del Mar, CA.

Keirsey, D. (1998) *Please Understand Me II: Temperament, Character, Intelligence*. Prometheus Nemesis, Del Mar, CA.

B.W. Tuckman

Tuckman identified four stages of team development, starting from its formation through to its working effectively as a cohesive unit. The four stages are given in Table 8.1.

Tuckman suggests that some teams will move quickly through the early stages and start to perform at an early stage. Others will become bogged down in the storming stage where they may languish for some time. It is also possible to go back through the stages; for example, a change of task, which requires a whole new method of working, or a change of group personnel, might lead a performing team back into the storming stage. Some groups, such as organizational departments, may go on for a very long time, simply changing the members from time to time. Others, such as project teams, may enter a fifth stage and actually disband when the job is complete.

Clearly, for teams in the forming and storming stage, team-building and development activities might be essential.

Table 8.1

Stage	Behaviors demonstrated
Forming – when the team first comes together	Members very tentative; not giving much away about themselves; over-polite to each other; watching each other
Storming – when conflicts arise	Conflict between members about how things should be done; some may leave; leadership contests; team bogged down
Normingn – when the team settles down to business	Organization; rules, systems, and procedures agreed; focus on the task ahead
Performing – when the team really begins to shine and achieve results	Members get to know each other and their skills; feedback given and accepted; trust builds between members; delegation of tasks; focus on people development as well as the task

Highlights

Articles:

"Developmental sequences in small groups," *Psychological Bulletin*, **63** (1965), American Psychological Association.

Meredith Belbin

Meredith Belbin has demonstrated that, apart from a person's functional role that they will have at work, they will also have a natural role that they will adopt when working in teams.

He argues that each role will have particular strengths that it will bring to the team, but also allowable weaknesses. He suggests that the latter are not worked on with a view to eradicating them, because they are the opposite side of the strength, which may, then, also be lost. Rather, the weaknesses should be managed by ensuring that a person is not put in a position where it will be a problem. He identified nine team roles, which we met in Chapter 3, and which are set out here in Table 8.2, along with their allowable weakness:

Table 8.2

Role	Strengths	Allowable weakness
Coordinator	Invites contributions	May be manipulative
Shaper	Drives, issues challenges	Quick to anger
Plant	Generates ideas	Not very practical
Implementer	Turns ideas into action	Possibly inflexible
Completer/finisher	Finishes the job off	Tends to worry
Team worker	Creates harmony	Not very decisive
Resource investigator	Excellent at networking	Quick to lose interest
Monitor/evaluator	Ensures all options considered	Not very motivational
Expert	Has specific knowledge	Knowledge may be of limited application

Belbin recognizes that a group of nine people would be unwieldy, so he recommends that people double up on some roles, leaving a team of three to five people. Some people have more than one natural role, while other people also have secondary roles which they can perform if needed. There will also be roles which they should avoid taking on.

Belbin has produced a software program which enable people to find out their natural team roles.

He argues that, if a team is to be effective, then all of the roles must be represented and that people who are responsible for improving and developing team performance need to be aware of this.

Highlights

Books:

Management Teams: Why they succeed or fail (1981) Butterworth-Heinemann, Oxford.
Team Roles at Work (1993) Butterworth-Heinemann, Oxford.

Changing the Way We Work (1997) Butterworth-Heinemann, Oxford.
Beyond the Team (2000) Butterworth-Heinemann, Oxford.
Managing Without Power (2001) Butterworth-Heinemann, Oxford.

Software

Interplace software and associated documentation and video, which allows people to identify their team roles; the program has many uses over and above this.

Donald L. Kirkpatrick

Donald Kirkpatrick is a former president of the American Society for Training and Development. He is the professor of the Management Institute, University of Wisconsin, a consultant, and an author. He set out a system in the 1960s for evaluating the effect of training and development, as we saw in Chapter 3. The four levels that he identified are still used by a huge number of organizations today. Table 8.3 shows some of the factors that organizations take into account.

We have already seen, in Chapters 6 and 7, how these can be applied and we will also see them in Chapter 10.

Donald Kirkpatrick's Website, as shown below, offers a wide range of training and development services, including training seminars and evaluation tools.

Highlights

Books:

Evaluating Training Programs: The Four Levels (1998) Berret-Koehler, San Francisco, CA.
Techniques for Evaluating Training Programs (1975) ASTD, Alexandria, CA.

Website:

Kirkpatrick Human Resource Management Training:
   www.management-inventories.com.

Table 8.3

Evaluation level	Key factors for the organization
Reaction – how do people feel during and immediately after the training?	Was the event: » enjoyable » interesting » stimulating » eye opening?
Learning – how much have they learned in terms of knowledge skills and attitudes?	Have they been introduced to new concepts? Has their knowledge increased? Have their attitudes changed?
Performance – what are they now doing differently as a result of the learning experience?	Have they transferred the learning to the workplace in the form of changed attitudes and behaviors? Can they cascade the learning to others in the team?
Organizational results – what additional benefits has the organization gained?	Can the new behaviors be translated into better results for the company? Was the training focused in the right areas? Are there other areas of the organization that could also benefit?

Peter Honey

Peter Honey, of Peter Honey Learning, is a well-known writer on training. He and Alan Mumford identified the four main learning styles which we met in Chapter 3. They argue that different people have different preferences for the way in which they learn. They will, therefore, learn more easily with some methods than with others, as shown in Table 8.4.

They produced a learning styles questionnaire, which enables learners to identify which is their preferred style.

Table 8.4

Style	Learn best:	Learn least:
Activists	when getting involved in an activity	in passive situations
Reflectors	when allowed to observe and reflect	when not allowed time to reflect before tackling a situation
Theorists	when they can think through experiences and develop concepts and theories	when they have no previous concepts or ideas to guide them
Pragmatists	when they can test out ideas in a real-life situation	when they are working in situations which they regard as unreal and having no link with their own work

Peter Honey has now produced a training styles questionnaire which enables trainers to identify their training styles. He has also developed The Learning Series, which is an integrated range of electronic products aimed at helping people to become more effective learners.

He writes articles which continually come up with innovative approaches, an example being "The changing face of learning" in which he suggests that learning should be tailored to individuals and provided for them when and how they can best take advantage of it. He suggests that learning should be:

» JIT – just in time
» JFM – just for me
» JWIN – just what I need
» IYF – in your face.

He produces a Web newsletter, which is available through his Website.

Highlights
Books:

A Manual of Learning Styles, with A. Mumford, (1986) Peter Honey Learning, Maidenhead.

Articles:

"The changing face of learning"
"An Identikit picture of a life long learner"
"Trainer styles"

Products:

The Learning Series
Learning styles questionnaire
Training styles questionnaire

Website:

Articles and products are on Peter Honey's Website at peterhoney.com.

Tony Buzan

Tony Buzan is famous for his many books about increasing the use of one's brain. He developed the use of mind mapping as a way of increasing a person's creativity. The technique can be used for a range of activities, including:

» preparing reports
» preparing presentations
» problem solving
» writing articles or books.

In this technique, you start off with a basic concept or idea, which you set out in the middle of the page, as in Fig. 8.2.

As related concepts come into your mind you jot them down showing links to the main idea and also links to each other. In this way, you can build up a cluster of interrelated ideas.

Highlights
Books:

The Mind Map Book: How to Use Radiant Thinking to Maximize Your Brain's Untapped Potential, with Barry Buzan (1996) Plume, London.

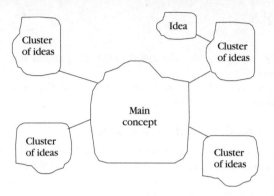

Fig. 8.2

Make the Most of Your Mind (1986) Simon and Schuster, London.
Use both Sides of Your Brain (1991) E P Dutton, London.
Brain Sell: Harnessing the Selling Power of your Whole Brain, with
   Richard Israel (1996) McGraw-Hill, London.

Stephen Covey

Stephen Covey has written many books on self-development. His *7 Habits of Highly Effective People* is a bestseller. In it he identifies three main strands.

» **Personal** – in which he looks at being proactive and focusing on the things that are most important to you.
» **Interaction** – in which he searches for win–win situations and clear communications with other people.
» **Renewal** – in which he stresses the need to keep your mind and body in good health while you achieve the first two.

In short, self-growth is important and you have to look after yourself while you do it. The analogy he uses is making sure you remember to "sharpen the saw."

Highlights

Books:

The 7 Habits of Highly Effective People (1994) Simon and Schuster, London.

Living the Seven Habits: Stories of courage and Inspiration (1999) Simon and Schuster, London.

Richard Bandler and John Grinder

Richard Bandler and John Grinder were the first to introduce the concept of neuro-linguistic programming (NLP) that we mentioned in Chapter 3.

The three elements of NLP are as follows.

» **Neuro** – which considers our brain patterns and the ways in which we prefer to communicate. Some people, for example, prefer to visualize the world, others prefer to hear it, while yet others prefer to touch it.

» **Linguistic** – refers to our speech patterns, which will be linked to the way in which we prefer to communicate. Phrases for the preferences mentioned above might include:
  » I see what you mean
  » I like the sound of that
  » I think I'm getting the feel of this now.

  The different preferences might be evident in the way a person asks for a report from someone else on a task they have been carrying out on their behalf:
  » Can you show me how far you've got?
  » Can you tell me what you've done so far?
  » How did you handle this aspect?

  NLP suggests that we should mirror the preferred methods of those with whom we are communicating, because, if one person is "seeing" while the other is "hearing," they are not really communicating at all.

» **Programming** – suggests that, from our earliest days, we become programmed to respond to certain events. Some people can't start work until they've had a cup of tea or coffee, for example. Well, if we can be programmed, we can also reprogram ourselves and change the ways in which we react. Thus, a person who usually writes good reports might feel great concern every time they submit one at work because someone, way back in time, once criticized one of their reports in a destructive way. By focusing on their best report and the best feedback they were ever given about it they can reprogram themselves to feel really good about the process.

NLP puts all of these factors together to:

» improve a person's communication with others;
» remove personal barriers; and
» build self-belief.

It is quite a complex approach and training programs are offered by many companies, either:

» to train people to adopt the approach; or
» to train people to be able to train other people.

Highlights

Books:

The Structure of Magic: A Book about Language and Therapy (1990) Science and Behavior Books, Palo Alto, CA.

The Structure of Magic II: A Book about Communication and Change (1980) Science and Behavior Books, Palo Alto, CA.

Reframing: Neuro-Linguistic Programming and the Transformation of Meaning, with Connirae Andreas (1989) Real People Press, Moab, UT.

Resources

Sets out the best resources for training and development, including:

» books and articles
» Websites
» magazines
» institutes.

BOOKS

Armstrong, M.A. (2000) *Handbook of Personnel Practice*. Kogan Page, London.

Bandler, R. & Grinder, J. (1980) *The Structure of Magic II: A Book about Communication and Change*. Science and Behavior Books, Palo Alto, CA.

Bandler, R. & Grinder, J. (1990) *The Structure of Magic: A Book about Language and Therapy*. Science and Behavior Books, Palo Alto, CA.

Bandler, R., Grinder, J. & Andreas, C. (1989) *Reframing: Neuro-Linguistic Programming and the Transformation of Meaning*. Real People Press, Moab, UT.

Belbin, R.M. (1981) *Management Teams: Why they succeed or fail*. Heinemann, Oxford.

Belbin, R.M. (1993) *Team Roles at Work*. Butterworth-Heinemann, Oxford.

Belbin, R.M. (2000) *Beyond the Team*. Butterworth-Heinemann, Oxford.

Briggs-Myers, I. & McCaulley, M.H. (1985) *Manual: A Guide to the Development and Use of the Myers Briggs Type Indicator*. Consulting Psychologists Press, Palo Alto, CA.

Briggs-Myers, I. & Myers, P. (1980) *Gifts Differing*. Consulting Psychologists Press, Palo Alto, CA.

Brinkerhoff, R. (1988) *Achieving Results from Training*. Jossey-Bass, San Francisco, CA.

Buzan, Tony (1986) *Make the Most of Your Mind*. Simon and Schuster, London.

Buzan, Tony (1991) *Use both Sides of Your Brain*. E P Dutton, London.

Buzan, T. & Buzan, B. (1996) *The Mind Map Book: How to Use Radiant Thinking to Maximize Your Brain's Untapped Potential*. Plume, London.

Buzan, T. & Israel, R. (1996) *Brain Sell: Harnessing the Selling Power of your Whole Brain*. McGraw-Hill, London.

Cartwright, R., Collins, M., Green, G. & Candy, A. (1993) *In Charge of Yourself*. Blackwell, Oxford.

Covey, S.R. (1990) *The 7 Habits of Highly Effective People*. Simon and Schuster, London.

Covey, S.R. (1999) *Living the Seven Habits: Stories of courage and inspiration*, Simon and Schuster, London.

Gaines Robinson, D. & Robinson, J. (1989) *Training for Impact*. Jossey-Bass, San Francisco, CA.

Hamblin, A.C. (1974) *Evaluation and Control of Training*. McGraw-Hill, Maidenhead.

Handy, C. (1976) *Understanding Organisations*. Penguin, London.

Handy, C. (1989) *The Age of Unreason*. Business Books, London.

Herzberg, F. (1966) *Work and the Nature of Man*. Staples Press, New York.

Honey, P. & Mumford, A. (1986) *A Manual of Learning Styles*. Peter Honey Learning, Maidenhead.

Huczynski, A. & Buchanan, D. (2000) *Organizational Behavior*. Pearson, London.

Kakabadse, A., Ludlow, R. & Vinnicombe, S. (1988) *Working in Organizations*. Penguin, London.

Keirsey, D. (1987) *Portraits of Temperament*. Prometheus Nemesis, Del Mar, CA.

Keirsey, D. (1998) *Please Understand Me II: Temperament, Character, Intelligence*. Prometheus Nemesis, Del Mar, CA.

Keirsey, D. & Bates, M. (1984) *Please Understand Me: Character and Temperament Types*. Prometheus Nemesis, Del Mar, CA.

Kirkpatrick, D.L. (1975) *Techniques for Evaluating Training Programs*. ASTD, Alexandria, CA.

Kirkpatrick, D.L. (1998) *Evaluating Training Programs: The Four Levels*. Berret-Koehler, San Francisco, CA.

Kolb, D. *et al.* (1979) *Organisational Psychology: An Experimental Approach*. Prentice Hall, Englewood Cliffs, NJ.

McGregor, D. (1960) *The Human Side of Enterprise*, McGraw-Hill, New York.

O'Connor, J. & Seymour, J. (1994) *Training with NLP*. Thorsons, London.

O'Connor, J. & Seymour, J. (2000) *Introducing Neuro Linguistic Programming: Psychological Skills for Understanding and Influencing People*. Thorsons, London.

Pavlov, I.P. (1941) *Conditional Reflexes and Psychiatry* (trans. and ed. W.H. Grant). International Publishers, New York.

Peters, T. (1987) *Thriving on Chaos*. Pan Books, London.

Peters, T. (1994) *Pursuit of Wow! Every person's guide to topsy-turvy times*. Macmillan, London.

Peters, T. & Waterman, R.H. (1982) *In Search of Excellence: Lessons from America's best-run companies*. Harper & Row, New York.

Phillips, J. (1991) *Handbook of Training Evaluation and Measurement Methods*. Gulf Publishing, Houston, TX.

Piaget, J. (1928) *Judgement and Reasoning in the Child*. Harcourt Brace Jovanovich, New York.

Skinner, B.F. (1953) *Science and Human Behavior*. Macmillan, New York.

Skinner, B.F. (1961) *Analysis of Behavior*. McGraw-Hill, New York.

Torrington, D. & Hall, L. (1998) *Personnel Management*. Simon and Schuster, London.

Trompenaars, F. (1993) *Riding the Waves of Culture*. Economist Books, London.

Watson, J.B. (1930) Behaviorism, 2nd edn. University of Chicago Press, Chicago, IL.

Whetton, D., Cameron, K. & Woods, M. (1994) *Developing Management Skills for Europe*. HarperCollins, London.

ARTICLES

Luft, J. & Ingham, H. (1955) "The Johari window: a graphic model of interpersonal awareness." In: *Proceedings of the Western Training Laboratory in Group Development*. UCLA, Los Angeles.

Maslow, A. (1943) "A theory of human motivation," *Psychological Review*, **50** (4).

Mintzberg, H. (1975) "The manager's job: folklore and fact," *Harvard Business Review*, **53**.

Tuckman, B.W. (1965) "Developmental sequences in small groups," *Psychological Bulletin*, **63**.

Stephen M. Brown, who is dean of the Center for Adult Learning and professor of management and education at Lesley College, Cambridge, MA, has articles on evaluation on a very interesting Website at: www.ktic.com.

G. Green and B. Green have written an article on coaching styles in the Autumn 2001 issue of *Training and Competence Magazine*.

L. Horridge, of TBO (UK) PLC, has written a series of three introductory articles on NLP:

» "How to change your outlook," Spring 98 edition of *Outlook Magazine* (now *Training and Competence News*)
» "Changing through NLP," Summer 1998 edition of *Outlook Magazine*
» "Changing through NLP," Autumn 1998 edition of *Outlook Magazine*.

P. Honey has several new articles:

» "The changing face of learning"
» "An Identikit picture of a life long learner"
» "Trainer styles."

All are available from Peter Honey's Website at peterhoney.com.

USEFUL WEBSITES

Blackboard: Blackboard.com
Peter Honey: peterhoney.com
D. Keirsey: keirsey.com
D.L. Kirkpatrick: www.management-inventories.com
Leonard Cheshire Workability Project: Jobability.com
R. Meredith Belbin: belbin.com
National Training Awards: www.NationalTrainingAwards.com
WorkSmart: WorkSmart.com

For sites offering consultation on Myers Briggs testing: search on Myers–Briggs, which will produce a significant list of companies offering their services.

Companies and authorities whose Websites have been useful in researching this text include:

American Airlines: www.amrcorp.com
British Airways: www.britishairways.com
Chartered Insurance Institute: www.cii.co.uk
Commonwealth Bank of Australia: www.commbank.com
Egg: www.egg.com

ExxonMobil: www.exxonmobil.com
Financial Services Authority: www.fsa.gov.uk
Financial Services National Training Organization: www.fsnto.org.uk
Ford Motor Co.: www.ford.com
Lockheed Martin: www.lockheedmartin.com
McDonald's: www.mcdonalds.com
NATS Ltd: www.nats.co.uk
Pepsi Cola: www.pepsico.com
PowerGen: www.powergen.com
Qantas: www.qantas.com
Rolls-Royce: www.rolls-royce.com
Singapore Airlines: www.singaporeair.com

MAGAZINES AND JOURNALS

Australian Training, Australian National Training Authority, AMP Place, 10 Eagle Street, Brisbane, Queensland 4000, Australia

British Journal of Educational Psychology, St Andrews House, 48 Princess Road East, Leicester LE1 7DR, UK

Creative Training Techniques Newsletter, Bill Communications, 50 S. Ninth Street, Minneapolis, Minnesota, USA

Human Resources Development International, Routledge Journals Dept, 29 West 35th Street, New York, NY 10001-2299, USA

Human Resource Development Quarterly, American Society for Training and Development, 350 Sansome Street, San Francisco, California, USA

International Journal of Training and Development, Blackwell Publishers, 108 Cowley Road, Oxford OX4 1FH, UK

LearningCurve, from International Data Corporation, 5 Speen Street, Framingham, Massachusetts, USA

New Directions in Program Evaluation, School of Education, Greensboro, North Carolina, USA

Performance Improvement, International Society for Performance Improvement, 1300 L Street NW, Suite 1250, Washington DC, USA

Training and Competence News (formerly Outlook Magazine), 15 Nash Lane, Freeland, Witney, Oxon, OX29 8HS, UK

trainingmag.com, an online training magazine available by subscription

INSTITUTES AND TRAINING BODIES

Chartered Institute of Banking, UK
Chartered Insurance Institute, UK
Financial Services National Training Organization, UK
Human Resources Institute, New Zealand
Institute of Personnel Management
Irish Management Institute
Malaysian Institute of Training and Development
Management Training and Development Institute
Manufacturing Management and Technology Institute
National Training Awards, UK
New York Institute of Finance
New York Training Institute for NLP

Ten Steps to Making the Concepts Work

Provides ten key steps to make the concepts work.

1 Identify the knowledge, skills, and attitudes needed to carry out the job or range of jobs.
2 Carry out an analysis of the current level of knowledge, skills, and attitudes, and establish the training gap.
3 Set priorities.
4 Identify training objectives.
5 Decide how success will be evaluated.
6 Set out individual action plans.
7 Identify the technology.
8 Identify training providers.
9 Deliver the training.
10 Evaluate success.

In the previous chapters, we have examined a number of concepts that help us to understand the value of both training and development and how they can best be carried out. In this chapter we will look at ten key steps that need to be taken to ensure they are carried out effectively and that they do, after all, result in the benefits that the organization expected.

The steps can be used in any organization:

» commercial or not-for-profit
» huge, medium, or tiny
» global or insular;

and at any level in it:

» strategic
» departmental
» team;

even down to a single individual.

Most steps should be carried out in order, although steps 7 and 8, identifying the technology and the providers, can run in parallel or could even be decided very early on in the process.

In practice, once the process has begun, the key steps will be repeated in a continuous cycle, with the technology and training providers only changing when it is opportune to do so.

1. IDENTIFY THE KNOWLEDGE, SKILLS, AND ATTITUDES NEEDED TO CARRY OUT THE JOB OR RANGE OF JOBS

Of course, this assumes that we know what people are expected to do and achieve in their jobs. Yet this is not always as straightforward as it may seem. There are several reasons why what people are supposed to do may be unclear.

» Jobs change in response to a number of factors, including:
  » new products being developed;
  » old products being withdrawn;
  » structural changes in the organization; and

» changes to legislation.
» Current job specifications may not be regularly updated; after all, it is impossible to issue new job specifications after every slight change.
» Job specifications may not exist; some organizations don't believe in them.
» Responsibilities may increase through empowerment (job enrichment).
» Some jobs, especially new ones, just grow (job enlargement).

Clearly, it is important that a regular review of what people actually do and what they are responsible for is carried out, so that any additional knowledge, skills, or attitudes that might be needed can be identified and addressed. If this is not done, as the job changes, a training gap will begin to grow and the person will not be able to carry out their job effectively.

In some jobs there are few or even no clear core routines. Charles Handy, in the *Age of Unreason* (1989), talks of the doughnut: the hole in the middle represents a person's main activities and responsibilities, while the outer ring represents additional responsibilities which may be less clear. Some jobs will have a clear set of tasks in their core, with fewer, less clear responsibilities in the ring. Others will have a very small set of core tasks and a large outer ring of more nebulous responsibilities.

Take a politician, for example!

What would their core activities be? Who could set a boundary on the tasks they may need to do in the outer ring?

The same points might apply to a PA in a large organization, who may have very few specified responsibilities, but might be expected to get involved in just about everything.

For these types of jobs, it may be more difficult to identify the knowledge, skills, and attitudes that are needed.

Once the key tasks and responsibilities have been identified as far as they can be, it is necessary to work out the levels of knowledge, skills, and attitudes that are required to carry them out effectively. We saw some examples in our section on competency frameworks in Chapter 6.

At this stage, it is also necessary to decide how detailed the analysis is going to be. Is the organization going for a complete competency framework or does it want a less formal system? Is the analysis going to be organization-wide or will it be confined to a department or a particular team?

Large organizations often seek the help of professional consultants when setting up large-scale competency frameworks.

2. CARRY OUT AN ANALYSIS OF THE CURRENT LEVEL OF KNOWLEDGE, SKILLS, AND ATTITUDES, AND ESTABLISH THE TRAINING GAP

This step follows logically from the first. We need to find out what the current levels of knowledge, skills, and attitudes are, so that we can establish the gap.

This will usually be carried out during performance reviews or through feedback sessions, though it could be carried out as a one-off exercise if a competency framework is being set up. We mentioned in Chapter 6 a benchmarking process in which employee and manager agree a rating for each of the knowledge, skills, and attitudes that are needed, which is then compared to the level that is required to carry out the job effectively.

As we saw in Chapter 4, there are now some very sophisticated tracking systems like Work Smart that can be used to feed in and track the level of competence throughout the organization.

3. SET PRIORITIES

Once the gaps are found, we need to address them. However, there may not be the resources available to address them all at one. This means that training and development needs may have to be prioritized.

If a new product is being rolled out, ensuring that sales staff gain the knowledge required before it hits the market may be more important than developing their forecasting techniques, though the latter may well become a priority once the new product is launched.

New technology can be enormously helpful here, because methods such as CD-ROM computer-based training or Internet/intranet packages may enable a lot of people to be trained at the same time with minimal impact on resources.

Of course, there may not be a gap and we may have a team of people who are working extremely effectively. If this is the case, we need to consider motivation theories like those of Maslow and Herzberg, whom we met in Chapter 2, and think of how we can stretch the people so that they continue to grow. For these people we will be seeking development opportunities rather than addressing training needs.

4. IDENTIFY TRAINING OBJECTIVES

Now that we know where the gaps are and have set out our priorities, we need to identify what we want to achieve. Clearly, we want to close the training gap and the first step is to define what the training gap is in terms that can be understood and managed.

For our new product, which we mentioned in step 3, we could suggest that:

> We want to ensure that, by the end of July, each member of our sales team can explain the benefits of our new product to a potential customer, with the result that they sell the product successfully and meet their sales targets.

If we work in a travel agency and we find that some team members are not quoting the correct fares, leading to complaints when the customer is subsequently charged the correct, higher fare by another team member, our training objectives might be:

> We want to ensure that, by the end of May, each team member can quote the correct fare, leading to an increase in customer satisfaction and a decrease in customer complaints.

If we are in financial services and we find that customer applications forwarded by some members of the team are being rejected by head office because they are incorrectly completed, our training objectives might be:

> We want to ensure that, by the end of June, all team members can satisfactorily complete the application forms, with the result that none are rejected and the customer's transaction is

completed without delay, leading to customer satisfaction and fewer complaints.

We can set training objectives at any level: individual and team as in the latter two examples, or departmental as in the first example; or we can set them for the organization as a whole. In a case study in Chapter 7 we even saw how they can be applied to a whole industry.

5. DECIDE HOW SUCCESS WILL BE EVALUATED

This stage should really be carried out in conjunction with the previous one. By setting out measurable objectives, we have already begun to think about what success will look like.

We need to ensure that we have systems in place to monitor progress toward that success. In short, we need to be sure about when that particular type of training has been successfully completed and we can, therefore, stop doing it and move on to another of our priorities that we identified in stage 3 above. We saw, in Chapters 6 and 8, that there are several aspects to the evaluation process and the success of our training effort can be measured in several different ways; we will look at these in more detail in step 10.

Here, we can consider how to evaluate the objectives we set out in the previous step.

For our new products we could use any of these methods:

» measure initial sales;
» seek feedback from customers;
» ask for a presentation from the individual;
» monitor subsequent sales figures; or
» observe the person in a sales interview.

In our travel agency we could:

» list the number of related complaints/compliments;
» record the number of errors; or
» observe the person or listen in to telephone interviews.

In our financial services company we could:

» monitor complaints;
» measure the response time between application and contract;

» record the number of rejected forms; or
» spot check a sample before it goes to head office.

6. SET OUT INDIVIDUAL ACTION PLANS

When the training gap for an individual is identified, we can work out an individual action plan with them. This will set out:

» how the need was recognized – for example, it might have arisen from a:
  » customer complaint
  » failure to reach targets
  » regular review meeting
  » observation;
» the extent of the gap and the measure of success;
» the activities that will be used to address the needs;
» the timescales; and
» the date of the next review meeting to discuss progress.

We can use the same process for identifying development needs. A person's individual development plan may contain several action plans each aiming to address different training or development needs.

As we saw in Chapter 6, coaching on a one-to-one basis can be very useful in supporting a person through their development plan. A coach might also be able to help the person find the best training method, or combination of methods, to achieve their training objectives and to suit their learning style. In our examples above we could use any combinations of the following methods.

» Sales team – briefing or demonstration, question and answer session, group discussion, role play, video.
» Travel agency – short course, role plays, case studies, self-study.
» Financial services – short course, instruction by coach, practice form completion.

Once a need is met, it can be signed off. It can be a very good idea for the individual to file or record the activities concerned in their development file, because it will allow them to reflect back, over a period of time, on their development within the organization.

7. IDENTIFY THE TECHNOLOGY

This step can be carried out in parallel with the other steps mentioned above. As soon as training and development needs are identified, organizations can begin to plan how they will address them and take into account the current technology available.

We saw, in Chapters 4 and 5, that there is a wealth of options available, using either new or old technology. Flip charts are still a very useful medium, even though there are higher tech replacements in the form of electronic whiteboards, for example.

The key factors in deciding which technology to use will include the following.

» Relevance to the learning opportunity – a demonstration video sent out via an organization's intranet might not allow sufficient group interaction.
» Likely effectiveness – a lecture might not be as stimulating as a small briefing session allowing questions and answers.
» Familiarity – if the learners are unfamiliar with the technology, it might stand in the way of their learning; for example, when Microsoft PowerPoint was first used in training, many people were so fascinated with the new technology that they missed out on the message it was delivering. Another factor is: do trainers themselves need to be trained in its use?
» Convenience – can it easily be moved to where it needs to be?
» Cost – is it value for money? The good point here is that new technology is relatively cheap once the hardware such as computers is available.
» Availability – will it be available when you need it? Videos, for example, are notorious for being double booked.
» Compatibility – is the equipment that you intend to use compatible with the equipment at the venue where the training will take place? Video systems, for example, are different in various parts of the world. Is the computer system that is available powerful enough to run your complex training program?

8. IDENTIFY TRAINING PROVIDERS

Like the previous step, this can be carried out at any time during the process. There are several options, each of which has attractions depending upon the situation.

» In-house trainers/coaches/materials – are effective if the organization has its own specialist training department. They will have knowledge of the organization and its culture, and will be aware of any current issues. Materials can be tailored to the organization's specific requirements.

» External training company – can provide trainers, coaches, and/or materials. Most professional training companies can provide experienced people who can very quickly become acquainted with the organization, its culture, and the key issues of the day. They will often have experience of working with a wide range of organizations, which can add a useful perspective to the training.

» In-house/training company partnerships – are possible in which external trainers use materials designed in-house, or in-house trainers use materials designed by external training companies.

» Universities, colleges, and institutes – are necessary if professional qualifications are desired.

Clearly, one of the key factors will be whether the organization has sufficient expertise in-house to design and deliver training programs. Handy (1989) refers to Shamrock organizations which consist of three elements:

» the core – people employed by the organization full time;
» contracted services – people or organizations contracted in to carry out specific activities; and
» flexible workforce – consisting of part-time, flexible workers.

In many such organizations training and development come into the contracted services category and they no longer maintain training and development departments of their own. The key advantages of this approach are:

» they can buy in more or less according to their needs;
» they can access a wide variety of training and development to fit any need anywhere in the organization;
» they can use specialists whose business is training and development and who, therefore, have access to the latest technology and to skilled people; and
» they can gain access to the latest Internet programs.

Some organizations maintain their own small training and development department for core training needs, such as product training, and contract-in the rest.

9. DELIVER THE TRAINING

Once the programs are planned, both in terms of the training to be provided and the people who will benefit from it, they need to be delivered. The key factors here will be ensuring that:

» an appropriate venue is available – and is not double booked as can so often happen; where the training is held will have a significant effect on the success of a training event, for example a room with no external light can lead to people becoming tired, while a room with a superb or interesting view can result in people becoming distracted;
» equipment works – as we saw earlier in this chapter, there is a variety of equipment available; it must be in working order;
» trainers are provided – specific instructions about dates, times, location, and the equipment available should be given to them;
» learners are prepared – joining instructions are important setting out:
    » how to find the venue
    » what time to arrive
    » what they should bring with them
    » what preparatory work they should have carried out in advance;
» materials are available – handouts and workbooks should be available;
» quality of training is maintained – there are a variety of methods that can be used to ensure that the training quality remains high, including:
    » training and developing the trainers

» observing sessions and offering feedback
» using feedback forms effectively.

We will look at evaluation in step 10.

10. EVALUATE SUCCESS

It is very important to know how effective the training and development effort has been.

We saw, in Chapters 3 and 8, that Kirkpatrick and Hamblin identified five levels of evaluation. You need to decide what level(s) of evaluation you are going to focus on and decide how you will capture the information. We have set out the five levels in Table 10.1, with some possible options for establishing how effective the training has been.

Table 10.1

Reaction – how do people feel during and immediately after the training?	Feedback forms at the event
	Feedback forms shortly after the event
	Telephone follow-up after the event
Learning – how much have they learned in terms of knowledge skills and attitudes?	Discussions with manager/coach
	Tests
	Observation
Performance – what are they now doing differently as a result of the learning experience?	Discussions with manager/coach
	Observation
	Feedback from customers
	Feedback from colleagues
	Changes in procedures
Organizational results – what additional benefits has the organization gained?	Monitor effect on individual's objectives
	Monitor effect on organizational objectives
Ultimate value – has the training helped the organization meets its strategic mission and goals, in terms of profitability, growth, or survival?	Monitor effect on key objectives related to the mission, goals, and values of the organization

Where training has been found to be less effective than planned, action can be taken to redesign it.

KEY LEARNING POINTS

We have identified ten key steps to make training and development effective.

1 Identify the knowledge, skills, and attitudes needed to carry out the job or range of jobs.
2 Carry out an analysis of the current level of knowledge, skills, and attitudes, and establish the training gap.
3 Set priorities.
4 Identify training objectives.
5 Decide how success will be evaluated.
6 Set out individual action plans.
7 Identify the technology.
8 Identify training providers.
9 Deliver the training.
10 Evaluate success.

Frequently Asked Questions (FAQs)

Q1: What is the difference between training and development?

A: Training focuses on what people need to learn to do their current job. Development focuses on what they will need in future. You can find out more in Chapter 2.

Q2: I know what I want my team to learn, but what is the best method to use?

A: There are a wide variety of methods, each with their own advantages, which are discussed in Chapter 6.

Q3: What does competence mean?

A: It means having the necessary knowledge, skills, and attitudes to carry out your job effectively. It is covered in Chapters 2 and 6.

Q4: What is open learning?

A: A method in which the learner can work in their own time and at their own pace. It is covered in Chapters 2 and 6.

Q5: How can I work out whether the amount I'm spending on training and development in my company is worth it?

A: Evaluation is covered in Chapters 3, 6, and 10. It is also mentioned in a case study in Chapter 7.

Q6: What is a development plan?

A: A plan followed by an individual to ensure that all of their training and development needs are identified and addressed. It is covered in Chapter 6.

Q7: What does a mentor do?

A: Acts as a support and motivator to a learner. The main responsibilities are set out in Chapter 6.

Q8: What is meant by coaching?

A: There are several forms of coaching, which are set out in Chapter 6.

Q9: What is NLP?

A: Neuro-linguistic programming, a relatively new approach to learning, which is covered in Chapters 3 and 8.

Q10: What is a training needs analysis?

A: An analysis of the skills that a person needs to carry out their job effectively, compared to the skills they already have. The difference is the training gap. This is covered in Chapters 2 and 6.

Index